LITERATURE THROUGH PERFORMANCE

Grant McKernie portraying the Old Man or Death in "The Pardoner's Tale" in *A Canterbury Caper*.

LITERATURE THROUGH PERFORMANCE

Shakespeare's Mirror and A Canterbury Caper

Katherine H. Burkman

OHIO
UNIVERSITY
PRESS
ATHENS, OHIO

ISBN 0-8214-0365-6 Cloth
ISBN 0-8214-0384-2 Paper
Library of Congress Catalog Number 76-25615
Printed in the United States of America

For THE COLLECTION,

Lynn Morrow, Wayne Lawson,
Grant McKernie, Robert Boyer,
Holly Chapman, Tom Roulston,
Michael Hurwitz, and Creighton Miller

who created the scripts in this book with me and who performed them with elegance.

ACKNOWLEDGMENTS

At the Francis W. Parker School in Chicago, drama is an integral part of the educational process; I would like to thank the many teachers there who first made learning through dramatic performance an exciting and rewarding experience for me. I would also like to express my gratitude to William Ball, whose New York workshop on Shakespearean acting has been a major influence on my work and is everywhere evident in this book. I am indebted as well to Charlotte and Charles Krown for their support of THE COLLECTION and to The National Endowment for the Humanities for the two grants which supported an Ohio tour of *Shakespeare's Mirror* (1970) and the development of *A Canterbury Caper* in the context of a workshop on The Role of Dramatic Performance in Education (1972).

I am grateful to Houghton Mifflin Company for permitting me to extract the scenes and songs used in *Shakespeare's Mirror* from *The Riverside Shakespeare,* 1974, and to The Viking Press for permitting me to use Theodore Morrison's translation of *The Canterbury Tales* in *The Portable Chaucer,* 1949, as the basis for my dramatic adaptation of *The Canterbury Tales* in *A Canterbury Caper.* Professor Morrison's excellent suggestions on the Chaucer script were most helpful and most welcome. I am also grateful to Tom Berg for permitting me to use his picture of Grant McKernie performing in *A Canterbury Caper.*

Finally, I am most appreciative of Dean Howard Stein's, Professor James Davis', Dr. Joan Wolf's, and Jane Cottrell's helpful suggestions on the manuscript and of Barbara Austin's expert typing and good will.

CONTENTS

THE TEACHER AS ARTIST: AN INTRODUCTION

In one sense all good teaching is an art. In the words of Thomas J. Cottle in his book, *Time's Children:* "It may be that the only fit teachers never teach but are artists, of the kind most blankly masked and least didactic."[1] But if good teaching is itself an art, teachers may also employ art for educational purposes in the more restrictive sense of the term. *Shakespeare's Mirror* and *A Canterbury Caper* were written to be performed by teachers who were themselves performing artists.

Although *Shakespeare's Mirror* and *A Canterbury Caper* were conceived as teaching scripts, they lend themselves to performance by professionals, amateurs, and students, as well as by teachers. The following account of the evolution of the scripts in their educational context is meant to be of help to all performers, whatever their backgrounds or purposes, as well as to nonperforming educators and students who are interested in the role of dramatic performance in education, or more specifically, in how to approach literature through performance.

In an immediate sense, *Shakespeare's Mirror* came into existence accidentally. I had previously directed four Ohio State University teachers in Harold Pinter's *The Collection* for a theater workshop. When asked if we would perform for some high school students in Kentucky, we decided that Pinter was not appropriate, and I scripted an initial version of *Shakespeare's Mirror* for the purpose. The enthusiastic response of the Kentucky students to the performance encouraged us to examine further possibilities in the script and in the entire concept of teaching through performance.

Thus, *Shakespeare's Mirror* became the impetus for the performers to organize themselves into a group of teacher/performers or teacher/artists as we subsequently referred to ourselves. Formed in 1969, THE COLLECTION, named after the first play we had worked on together, set out in 1970 on an Ohio tour of *Shakespeare's Mirror* under a grant from The National Endowment for the Humanities. In 1971, the group of performing teachers began work on *A Canterbury Caper,* which they further developed and performed in conjunction with a National Endowment for the Humanities sponsored workshop on The Role of Dramatic Performance in Education, taught by THE COLLECTION members in the summer of 1972.

Not unlike experiments in bringing the artist into elementary, high school, or college classrooms,[2] THE COLLECTION'S program on Shakespeare was an experiment in bringing to the public, both inside and outside the classroom, the talents of those who combine educational and artistic abilities. If a division must be made, the group of traveling players tended to think of themselves as teachers first, and then as performers, offering *Shakespeare's Mirror* as an educational experiment with the teacher as artist.[3]

The central theoretical basis of THE COLLECTION'S experiments with teaching literature through performance is the Aristotelian concept of drama as the imitation of action. Aristotle saw life as activity or process rather than as quality. He also noted man's natural inclination to learn about life through imitation. Poetry, he suggested, which includes all forms of literature and drama, springs partly from the "instinct of imitation" through which man "learns his earliest lessons." It also gives enjoyment because "no less universal is the pleasure felt in things imitated," the cause again being "that to learn gives the liveliest pleasure."[4] THE COLLECTION'S educational efforts were directed at using imitation and the writer/actor/audience interaction which is part of theatrical experience to involve the students in the action of literature, and to make them active participants in the aesthetic and educational experience.

Related to Aristotle's theories, and especially suggestive for the teacher who would use art to educate, are the aesthetic and educational theories of John Dewey. In *Experience and Education* and *Art as Experience* Dewey finds experience, which he defines as a doing and undergoing process, at the heart of education and aesthetics. According to Dewey, a picture hanging on a wall in a museum will have no aesthetic value in itself for a viewer any more than information handed down by authority will have any educational value in itself for a student. A person must enter into an active relationship with a work of art in order to perceive its value or imbibe its meanings, just as a student must enter into an active relationship with the material he studies if he is to perceive its value or imbibe its meanings.[5] Recognizing the kinship between the interaction that live theater's imitation of an action produces and the interaction that is essential to live educational experience, the members of THE COLLECTION became convinced that a good aesthetic experience would itself be a good educational one.

Shakespeare's Mirror, then, only seemed to come into existence by chance; the choice of subject matter, the form of the script, and the shape it took in performance were grounded in well-defined philosophical and educational theories. Shakespeare was an ideal choice for our purposes with his view of the theater, expressed by Hamlet in his Advice to the Players, in which the goal of playing is "to hold as 'twere the mirror up to nature: to show virtue her feature, scorn her own image, and the very age and body of the time his form and pressure."[6] This partly medieval concept of the stage as an educational and moral tool, as well as a microcosm of life, builds on Aristotle's perception of the learning potential in the imitative process, even while the dynamics of Shakespeare's artistic mirror provide for the kind of participation and interaction that Dewey found essential to the aesthetic and educational experience. The image of the stage as mirror became central to the development of both our Shakespeare and Chaucer scripts.

In form, *Shakespeare's Mirror,* which takes some ninety minutes to perform, consists of a selection of scenes from Shakespeare's plays, connected by narrative and interspersed with song. The idea of drama as a mirror of life is established at the opening with Hamlet's Advice to the Players, while other selections disclose the way in which Shakespeare's art reflects life in all of its richness, depth, and variety. Four players may take all of the roles, performing against any simple background and using three stools and a box of properties for setting.

In keeping with its educational goals, the program's narrative does more than introduce the scenes; it comments on Shakespeare's art and develops the concept of it as a mirror of life. THE COLLECTION incorporated post-sessions into its performances as well, interchanges with the audience, in which they answered questions and posed some themselves. The goal was not only to bring Shakespeare and live theater to various audiences, but also to communicate to them what theater is and can be.[7]

In THE COLLECTION'S performances of the script four actors — three men and one woman — took all of the roles. Dressed in modern costumes, they moved to the box of properties to don a cloak, doff a jacket, or pick up a mug. They also took turns with the narrative, introducing the scenes and commenting briefly on some aspect of Shakespeare's art. After the opening song, taken from *Twelfth Night,* for example, which was sung by the actors moving through the aisles to the stage, an actor introduced Hamlet; and as he set the scene, he himself moved to one of the three stools to become one of the players whom Hamlet addresses. Similar efforts were continually made to keep the narrative moving so that it did not become isolated from the theatrics as a separate piece of teaching.[8]

Since the "mirror" concept is at the center of the script, we tried having the actors echo Hamlet's words about it. They sat there on their stools, ponderously reciting in unison: "Suit the action to the word, the word to the action, with this special observance, that you o'erstep not the modesty of nature: for any thing so o'erdone is from the purpose of playing, whose end, both at the first and now, was and is, to hold as 'twere the mirror up to nature."[9] Leaving this deadly recitation behind, the actors started clowning, picking up their stools, dancing about, and jazzing up the rhythms of the speech. The clowning was effective, and in about two hours we worked out the transition with jazz rhythms and dancing, the actors resetting the stage with the stools as they danced with them and preparing the stage for Jaques' "Ages of Man" speech from *As You Like It.* Hence, a good deal of the liveliness of the performance developed from what the actors discovered spontaneously in interaction with each other and the material.

The content of Shakespeare's plays and the precedent set by performance techniques in his own time demand another kind of interaction as well — that between actor and audience. In the "Ages of Man" speech that follows Hamlet's "Advice to the Players" speech, Shakespeare's often repeated image is expressed by the melancholy Jaques that "All the world's a stage, /And all the men and women merely players."[10] The stage, then, not only mirrors life; it becomes a metaphor for it. We are "merely players" to Jaques, and meaningless ones at that to the embittered Macbeth, or insubstantial theatrical illusions in the mind of Prospero. By implication then, life itself is no more lasting, meaningful, or real than stage life. On the more positive side, however, the identification of actor and audience by so many of Shakespeare's characters and of microcosm (Shakespeare's theater, significantly called The Globe) and macrocosm (those on the globe itself reduced to the role of actors) would seem to invite actor and audience to unite in the search for what is lasting and meaningful in life through art.

Thus united, the auditors as well as the actors who imitated them were cast in an active role in Shakespeare's theater, one that evidently they accepted and relished. The Elizabethan stage jutted out into the audience, some of whom were standing, the groundlings, some of whom sat in balconies above, some of whom may even have been sitting on the stage, and all of whom were doubtless vocal and restless. Their activeness may partly be the result of the proximity of actor to audience and the convention of the actor's addressing the audience directly in soliloquy as well as in aside, but the actor/audience interaction and the nature of the staging also reflect Shakespeare's constant identification of actor and audience. In *Through The Looking Glass* fashion, Shakespeare's stage as microcosm draws the audience as macrocosm into its life, with the actors releasing the audience only to get the response that gives them their life. For if the actors become a mirror for the audience, the audience's response operates as a mirror for the actors in which they may see the authenticity of their imitations as they take form.

THE COLLECTION'S various ways of interacting with the audience partly follow the precedent of Shakespeare's own time. Our actor playing Hamlet, for example, broke the gulf between the proscenium and the audience, now advising his fellow performers on how to act, now advising the audience directly as if they too were part of the scene. The actor playing Jaques also addressed the audience directly, assuming that they were the

Duke's men gathered in the forest. But the rejection of the modern convention of much modern stage and screen performance, in which the actor assumes that a wall separates him from the audience, in favor of the convention of the actor's admitting that the audience is there and addressing them directly is as fitting today as it was in the sixteenth century, largely because of the complex dynamics of Shakespeare's mirroring process.[11]

The three selections in *Shakespeare's Mirror* that follow "The Ages of Man" speech all serve as examples of ways in which Shakespeare invited the audience to use their imaginations actively; in each one the characters set their own stage with words. Hence, Lorenzo invokes the musical night for his love of Jessica in *The Merchant of Venice;* the misshapen monster, Caliban, responds to the music of *The Tempest's* desert island with a musically poetic appreciation; and Juliet, about to drink the sleeping potion in *Romeo and Juliet,* paints in her imagination the frightening burial chambers where she will awaken.

In working out this section of our script, we included some contemporary music; two of the actors serenaded Lorenzo and Jessica with the theme song from Zeffirelli's film of *Romeo and Juliet.* In the second section of the program we used the song "What a Piece of Work is Man" from the rock musical *Hair.* The use of this music, combined with some music from Shakespeare's time, the modern costumes, and periodic performing in the aisles were techniques that we employed to enhance Shakespeare's direct appeal to modern audiences. It should be stressed, however, that with the exception of the brief jazz treatment of "Suit the action to the word," we remained faithful to the language and the rhythms of Shakespeare throughout. If Hamlet truly speaks for Shakespeare when he adjures the actors to "Suit the action to the word, the word to the action" in order to reflect life accurately, in a sense he is equating the word with the action. Thus there is no other honest approach to Shakespeare than through the poetry. The timeless and hence contemporary appeal of Shakespeare lies mainly in the poetry itself; his music contains his meaning.

In an effort to make Shakespeare intelligible to their audiences, American actors often have a tendency to slow down the narration. They take long naturalistic pauses and they break up the designated rhythms in order to make the plays more "conversational" and less "poetic." The result is often both distorting and dull.

Shakespeare helps his actors more than most other playwrights because he gives them words and rhythm to express their thoughts and feelings and hence writes a good deal of what today we call "subtext" right into the text itself. For example, when Jaques goes from age to age of man providing us with images of man's condition, he need not pause to think of the next one. Jaques states at the outset that there are seven stages (he has obviously given them thought or he wouldn't frame them as seven), and he begins the description of all but one stage in midline. The actor's task here is not to pause to dream up each stage, but to move from one to the next in the continuous rhythms provided; and transitions in thought must be made *on* the line rather than between lines.[12]

The system is essentially an English one — listen if you will to recordings of Sir John Gielgud and Dame Edith Evans, or see the Canadian Stratford Company to hear it at work — but the main point is that it does work. The actor is not merely eliminating pauses; he is also keeping up with the Shakespearean character's usually fast thinking and agile mind, and he is inviting the audience to do the same. Members of that audience may, of course, lose words with this rapid pace; but they will do so anyway, and they are more apt to keep up with the meanings if the actors keep up the music.

The program was designed to move from its mirror concept (Hamlet, Jaques), to a concentration on how the poetry works to engage the imagination *(As You Like It, The Tempest, Romeo and Juliet),* to the variety of ways the "mirror" works. The next selections, taken from *Henry IV, Part I,* reveal Shakespeare's use of English history to reflect the present in the past, while selections from *The Tempest, Othello, As You Like It,* and *The Taming of the Shrew* demonstrate various ways in which Shakespeare approaches the question of love.

The *Henry IV* scenes were chosen partly in order to involve all of the actors, since the earlier selections were speeches, partly to give the different approaches to honor that are taken in the play, and also to return once more to the mirror image. While Shakespeare's play mirrors the present in the historical past, Prince Hal's play within the play, in which he and Falstaff improvise Hal's forthcoming meeting with his father, King Henry, mirrors his own future. Despite its ostensible lightheartedness, the imitative process is clearly educational for Prince Hal, helping him to acquire a sense of reality and an awareness of his future responsibilities.

Shakespeare, the consummate artist/teacher, who understood the combined educative and pleasurable aspects of the imitative process,[13] gave even more dimension to the mirror of his art through his frequent use of the play within the play. Like the more tragic Hamlet, continually improvising roles and seeking to grasp the nature of the action he must take through the presentation of a play, Prince Hal finds his way to mature action through the liberating effect of knowledge that comes through "playing." As the identifying audience, we too, of course, share in that liberating knowledge, learning as much from Falstaff's improvisations as Hal does, and learning as well from the role playing of Hal.

Even in Shakespeare's love scenes, the characters as well as the audience often become students. We witness the innocence of Ferdinand and Miranda's love at first sight through the somewhat suspicious eyes of Prospero and are convinced as he is of its worth and life-giving force. We listen with the Duke and Desdemona's enraged father to Othello's defense of his wooing of the fair maiden and with them must judge for ourselves of his tale of how the two lovers became each other's captives through the sharing of the Moor's tales of his romantic adventures. With Orlando we get a humorous and ironical view of love as a mad and consuming passion from the disguised Rosalind, though we see through her disguise and know that her teachings are but a test which will permit her, and us, to learn more of the constancy and worth of Orlando's love. Finally, as the mirror shifts to the physical and witty verbal battle of the sexes that rages between the shrewish Kate and her determined suitor, Petruchio, in *The Taming of the Shrew,* we may see the animal side of human nature (note the many images of animals in the scene as well as the behavior), the bawdy side of love, and the eternal power struggle between men and women, as familiar to us today as it was to Shakespeare in his time. There is, however, ample evidence in the play for this scene to be played as a teaching as well as a taming one, with Petruchio challenged as a teacher by his witty if shrewish pupil, and doubtless, like all good teachers, learning from the experience himself — as we do.

Following a brief intermission, the second half of the program explores Shakespeare's tragic world, beginning with scenes from *King Lear.* Despite the disintegration of character that Lear undergoes, which culminates in his agonized question, "Who is it that can tell me who I am?"[14] what Shakespeare mirrors in his tragic world is the hard-won self-knowledge of the hero. Although Lear's suffering through the events of the play leads him and us to that knowledge, it comes too through the jesting, quipping, singing Fool, whom we see instructing the King on his foolishness, not this time through a play within a play, but certainly through theatrics within the theater. Tragic recognition provides knowledge and hence pleasure for the audience, since Lear's growing insights, like those of any great tragic hero, reflect the mysterious nature of all of our beings.

The script moves then from Lear's tragic plight to the intentional evil of Macbeth and Lady Macbeth, and includes Macbeth's speech of despair at the cost of the dehumanization the couple has undergone. The following scene between Hamlet and Polonius focuses on the way Shakespeare mirrors the tragic and comic in combination, while the song from *Hair,* using Hamlet's sensitive and abstracting intelligence, explores the nature of man in the universe, the theatrical Globe and the spinning one, the enormous possibilities of life, and the dust to which we all return. The concluding scene from *A Midsummer Night's Dream,* with its wistful speculation about the nature of human existence, completes the program, the actors exiting through the audience, singing the song with which they had begun.

THE COLLECTION learned much about *Shakespeare's Mirror* as they continued to develop it on tour and to respond to its reception by audiences that ranged from high school students to mental patients to university people. A question asked by a member of one of our university audiences in a post-session became of paramount interest to us on our tour: "How were we as groundlings?" Our interest in "groundling" reaction was based on our desire to gauge the educational success of the program, but interest in his question stemmed from our desire to bring about audience awareness of their own potentially active role in the theatrical experience. A student in another particularly responsive group refined the question; she wanted to know both how her high school friends were as an audience and whether their reactions affected the performance, which, of course, they had.

There was a general concern in the high schools about assembling large numbers of students; one school restricted the audience to honors students, while another held the program after school on a voluntary basis, with the principal and several teachers standing guard. The questions received from this latter group of some one hundred students were fairly typical of the ones we received in other post sessions. How could the actors "fit" so many roles? Were we professional actors? What else would we do in the future? How could they prepare themselves for careers as actors? The responses to the program were also typical. They had thought Shakespeare was boring, but he was fun. How wonderful for the actors to come in singing through the aisles and how surprising. How enjoyable it was to use their own imaginations rather than having lots of scenery, and how suspenseful live theater was in comparison to television.

The audiences did not always save their response for the post-sessions. In one high school where some eight hundred excited students gathered for a special day devoted to Social Studies and Humanities, when Falstaff went into the audience and asked the rhetorical questions in his "honor" speech, some students began answering the questions. By the end of the speech all eight hundred seemed to be responding in unison and the speech was greeted with wild applause, obviously for themselves as groundlings as well as for the actor playing Falstaff. In another school which housed a performance for several Head Start groups, when Petruchio pulled the still untamed Kate into a dip and gave her a kiss, a member of the audience yelled out, "Right-on," and brought down the house.

At both an Arts Festival performance and at recreation center performances we found that the program could hold rather young children who were in fact often more responsive than some of the more cynical teenagers. Some audiences were less articulate than others — the three senior citizens groups, for example, were enthusiastic about the program but unable to express why, and the silence of the patients at the mental institution was itself vocal. One young man wearing a peace sign pendant about his neck seemed afraid to look but obviously listened attentively throughout. Other audiences were extremely vocal, with one community audience engaging in a rather heated post-session debate on the tempo of the verse. A generation gap became evident as a retired drama teacher voiced criticism of our pace while younger teachers and students defended it as proper and a challenge to them to keep up. Their responses led to an excellent discussion about the rhythms of Shakespeare and techniques of presentation.

Perhaps our most peculiarly satisfying experience was our last one at a settlement house. A platform had been placed in a school yard, but there were no chairs, and when we arrived there was also no audience. As we put up the scenery, however, some children arrived on bikes, and we sent them off to invite their parents to return with them. When we began, a small group had assembled, and the children watched while sitting on their bikes, riding about when bored, returning when they thought something looked interesting. One little two-year-old crawled up on the platform and, included by the actors, became a delightful link between them and the audience.

Because questions and responses in the post-sessions were often about both the plays and about the acting in live theater, we felt that the program had realized its potential for teaching about Shakespeare and about the theater. The vocal response during the program as well as after it, also suggests its potential for the active audience response which is essential to the theatrical and educational experience.

We too learned as we made our tour. When playing before senior citizens, we were uncomfortably aware of all the references to age in the plays; when playing at a mental institution we became aware of all the images of madness; and the military references struck us as we played for some children of the military. As they went, the group also became more adept at handling different kinds of responses — at a recreation center where many small children attended they played for them, while the reactions of more sophisticated audiences helped them to discover and to play nuances of meaning of which they had been previously unaware.

Interested in sharing all that we had learned on tour and in encouraging other teachers to form similar teacher/artist groups for which they might develop scripts of their own, THE COL-

LECTION embarked on an NEH-sponsored workshop on The Role of Dramatic Performance in Education in the summer of 1972. While preparing for the workshop, we found that our goals became considerably broader as well as clearer. We still wished to explore ways in which the teacher/artist could help students experience and understand literature, with Shakespeare as the focal point, but we became interested in a performance-oriented approach to nondramatic as well as dramatic literature, and we enlarged our goals to encompass the involvement of students in performing as a way of learning about literature.[15]

Several of us had experimented over the years in our own classrooms with the use of student performance of nondramatic as well as dramatic literature. And of course stage and television adaptations of nondramatic literature are common enough, but there is also ample theoretical justification for approaching nondramatic literature through performance. Such critics as Kenneth Burke and Francis Fergusson are extremely convincing, for example, in their extension of Aristotle's concept of drama as an imitation of an action to nondramatic literature.[16] It would seem to follow from Aristotle's idea that life itself "consists in action, and its end is a mode of action, not a quality,"[17] that all of literature which imitates, reflects, and elucidates life for us may fruitfully be approached through active means, specifically through the activity of performance.

The essentially dramatic structure of *The Canterbury Tales,* perceived and explored by George Lyman Kittredge in *Chaucer and His Poetry,* derives partly from the interrelationships and interaction among the pilgrims on their journey. The pilgrims do not exist for the tales, but the tales for the pilgrims, Kittredge holds, in what he calls Chaucer's "micro-cosmology — a little image of the great world."[18] In order, then, to give life to what we became convinced was another potential theatrical microcosm, we selected five tales for dramatization, both for their potential for dramatic action and for their variety. We wished to avoid the overemphasis on the bawdy tales that had characterized a recent musical version of the *Tales* at the expense of capturing the many dimensions of Chaucer's world. We also dispensed with a connecting educational narrative, choosing to use only Chaucer himself to convey the experience of the literature. In that sense *A Canterbury Caper* became more of an artist/teacher's script than a teacher/artist's one.

Using only three ladders and a variety of pillows of different sizes and shapes for properties, THE COLLECTION achieved the portability of performance of *Shakespeare's Mirror*. As with the former program, such simplicity encouraged an active actor/audience relationship, with the actor making his demands on the audience's imagination.[19]

In order to infuse the narrative sections of *A Canterbury Caper* with life, and also because of the nature of the material within the narratives, the performance of the script was more physically active than the performance of *Shakespeare's Mirror*. Whereas economy of movement, suiting the action to the word, had been appropriate for Shakespeare, the Canterbury pilgrims seemed to demand an almost acrobatic life. The spring weather as setting, the journey, the humor, the various uses of ladders, pillows, and the body itself became the ingredients for a performance that was almost a dance.

The ladders were arranged to serve now as a bed, now as a window in "The Miller's Tale"; as a bier in "The Prioress' Tale"; or as a table and then a tree in "The Pardoner's Tale" as needed. Pillows became the bottle of poison and then the sword with which the roisterers fight in "The Pardoner's Tale," and were used as boat and oars in "The Miller's Tale" in the scene of imagined escape from the oncoming flood. They were used too as the hot poker Absolom wielded for his revenge, or even as a pillow itself for the sleeping Carpenter. Pillows were also heaped on the Wife of Bath so that she could emerge from them and begin her dramatic story.

The stage environment was also filled by the actors themselves, who became the animals in the barnyard setting of "The Nun's Priest's Tale," a forest through which the Knight moved seeking to find out what a woman most desires in "The Wife of Bath's Tale," and the headboard, an extremely active one, for the bed the Knight tried not to lie on with the Old Woman he married in return for the right answer in the same tale.

The use of ladders, pillows, and bodies as properties in *A Canterbury Caper* was designed, however, to serve the larger purpose of bringing Chaucer's vision of the pilgrims' world to life. We needed to explore the relationships of the story tellers to their stories as well as the relationship of pilgrim to pilgrim if the whole was to be dramatic and was to illuminate the literature. In *Shakespeare's Mirror* the actors had taken the many roles provided by the variety of scenes. Now the playing of roles within roles, a device that brought out the story teller-story relationship dramatically, presented a new challenge for the actors in terms of communicating Chaucer's meanings.

It seemed fitting, for example, for the Wife of Bath to play the role of the Old Woman in her own tale since the transformation of the ugly hag into a desirable beauty once she was given the reins of power by her reluctant husband was the poignantly impossible dream of the aging but lusty Wife herself.[20] Further dramatic dimension could be given to the Pardoner as well if he played the threatening role of the Old Man or Death in his tale of how the Old Man lures to their doom the greedy young men who would kill Death. Such doubling could suggest the potential spiritual death that lay within the Pardoner's own hypocritical and greedy soul, almost as if the Pardoner were the agent of retribution for sinners but also the incarnation of the results of such sin itself.

Dramatic solutions to the presentation of "The Prioress' Tale" included not only the Prioress doubling as the mother of the slain child, an obvious role for the Prioress' fantasies, but also the development of a movement concept of the whole in terms of children's games. The concept emerged from and was designed to reflect the Prioress' own childlike character and the rather innocent and simple view of good and evil that emerges in her tale.

The challenge in working out "The Nun's Priest's Tale" was to bring out the mock heroic style that is often so difficult to communicate to students in the classroom. The seriousness with which the actors created the barnyard and its animal inhabitants was of course the secret to success here as it is the means to any good comic effect. Since the juxtaposition of circumscribed animal world and high human passion and debate is the source of the humor, both had to be realized by the actors.

The actor playing Chaucer not only turned into the Miller as he described him getting ready to tell his tale; he also turned into the Carpenter who is the subject of "The Miller's Tale." Combined with the image of the characters "growing" into life as Chaucer delivers the opening of the Prologue, the playing of roles within roles in the whole program contributes to a sense of the constant birth of spring. The spirited initial entrance of the actors, interrupting the ponderous recitation of the Prologue in Middle English, and the final raucus overpowering of Chaucer's recantation by his own creations express the irrepressible good will and life of Chaucer's characters. Only the hypocrisy of the Pardoner presents any real threat to the salvation that the pilgrims desire, a hypocrisy so profound, as Chaucer had conceived it, that the Pardoner fools not the pilgrims so much as himself. He alone becomes lost in the pretense that Chaucer continually, lightheartedly, and compassionately exposes. Perhaps the acrobatic nature of THE COLLECTION'S performance of *A Canterbury Caper* grew out of the central action that unites it, which is to overcome death with the exuberance of wit and of love and of life.

To involve students even further in that action, members of THE COLLECTION have subsequently directed student performances of *A Canterbury Caper.*[21] But even as we were sharing our teacher-as-artist approach with the workshop participants for whom the Chaucer program was performed, our interest was already growing in the educational possibilities for the student-as-artist. We asked the teachers and prospective teachers of literature who were our students to engage in the kinds of learning activities in which we hoped they in turn would involve their students. These activities, all geared to approaching literature through performance, required them to be active as audience, as actors, and as writers. As audience, we invited them to our rehearsals of *Shakespeare's Mirror* which we revived for the workshop and to our rehearsals of *A Canterbury Caper* during which they could see THE COLLECTION struggle actively with the problems of bringing a nondramatic piece of literature into dramatic life—and of course they attended performances of the two works as well. As actors, we engaged them in improvisational exercises devised to approach dramatic and nondramatic literature; we asked them to perform speeches or scenes from the plays of Shakespeare; and we invited them to perform in a number of student-written scripts, somewhat on the order of our Shakespeare and Chaucer ones, which we asked each of them to create. Six of these scripts were selected for performance as the culmination of the workshop's activities.

The student, as Madeleine Grumet points out in *Toward a Poor Curriculum,* is not made, but is a maker, an artist.[22] Since all of our efforts as teacher/artists were aimed at encouraging students to play an active role as audience which would involve them in the experience of literature, it was but a short step to asking them to play the even more active roles of actor and writer in order to intensify their experience with literature.

Francis Fergusson in *The Idea of a Theater* indicates ways in which Aristotle's definition of drama as the imitation of an action is paralleled and elucidated by the acting theory of Constantin Stanislavski, which centers around the identification and playing of actions. Fergusson would have the reader develop what he calls a histrionic sensibility, the capacity to read a play imaginatively as potential performance, much as an actor or a director reads a play, or as a musician reads a musical score. Such a reading involves both a direct mimetic response and the grasping of the dramatic action that the playwright has imitated.[23]

Action, then, is imitated by the playwright, whom Aristotle described as a kind of actor himself,[24] played by the actor, and perceived imaginatively by the reader or the audience of a play. Involving the student in the experience of acting, whether in improvisations or in scene work, is but an extension of Fergusson's idea that we should read as actors do. Specific Stanislavski techniques that can help the student both act and read actively involve the perception of actions and their designation with infinitive phrases; finding a central action that the plot, characters, and thought of the play all imitate (in Stanislavski's terms, the superobjective); examining the given circumstances of the play out of which the action emerges; and relating oneself imaginatively to the characters and to those circumstances by asking yourself, What IF I were in that situation?[25]

All of these Stanislavski exercises may become tools of literary analysis for those who prefer to remain readers or audience, but we explored their possibilities both in terms of acting in class sessions and in relationship to the scripts that the students were writing. In order to improvise a tale from Chaucer, the students discovered that they needed to find the action that propelled them. The Knight in "The Wife of Bath's Tale," for example, needs *to seek the answer* to the question of what women most want, a seeking action. Knowing the given circumstances, the fact that he would lose his life if he did not find the answer within the year, influenced the intensity with which he searched, and knowing how close to the end of the year it was gave him even more means to imagine his state. Using other students as the woods through which he rode, and encouraging these human trees, animals, and such to become obstacles in his path provided further dramatic dimension for the search. Encouraging the actor to imagine what it would be like IF he were in such a situation, a task that involves introspection about one's own experience, also helped the actor (and would help the reader) to enter into the life of the character portrayed.

Other improvisational exercises, particularly those involving moving and behaving like animals, helped the students with their Shakespeare scene work. One student, who had been unable to grasp the rhythm or meaning of Shylock's "Hath a Jew Eyes" speech from *The Merchant of Venice* was able to grasp both by imitating a snake and spitting the lines out as he literally writhed on his belly on the floor. Another student developed an effective Hamlet in his scene with Ophelia by using the image of a fox.

Stanislavski techniques often involve working from the inside out, but we found value too in working from the outside in. As the students struggled with the same techniques of handling Shakespearean verse which THE COLLECTION employed in their preparation of *Shakespeare's Mirror,* they became more aware of the interrelationships between form and meaning than they could have become even as the most active of audiences.

From an educational point of view, such improvisation and scene work may be extremely profitable, even if it never leaves the audience of the classroom. Nevertheless, we did find another range of educational values for the student-as-artist by involving students in script writing and production before a larger audience. Rather than using the device of educational narrative as employed in *Shakespeare's Mirror,* the students tended to juxtapose materials either from a single author (e.g., Twain, Blake, Plath) or from a variety of authors writing on a particular theme (e.g., one script drew on a number of New England writers and was called *Seeing New Englandly.)* Some students chose to dramatize portions of novels such as Stern's *Tristram Shandy* or Kafka's *The Trial,* and there was even a script for young children called *Mother Goose and Her Children.*

In the writing and rewriting of the scripts, the central concept of dramatic action became as important as it was to THE COLLECTION in its performance approach to scripts. The author of a script on teenagers coming to terms with their world wrote: "If an action were to be ascribed to the script, I think it would be to discover some workable arrangement between the world and themselves: to perforce define themselves in their environment."

This definition of self in the environment or in the universe is, of course, what both art and education are about. But we may not simply see ourselves in the mirror of art. The learning process is a dynamic one, much like the acting exercise in which two students face each other and imitate each other's facial expressions and gestures in slow-motion, with neither a leader nor a follower designated.[26] The student, whether as actor, writer, or audience, must be active.

As teaching scripts, both *Shakespeare's Mirror* and *A Canterbury Caper* are designed to create active audiences and to involve the student in the experience of theater and of literature. Both scripts employ simple settings and properties, as well as multiple role playing, seeking through suggestion to awaken the audience's imagination and to invite both identification with the experience and participation in it. Because of the richness of vision and the many dimensions of the artistic mirrors of Shakespeare and Chaucer, such an experience may promote that special growth and learning that derives from the knowledge of self that is the object of all art.

SHAKESPEARE'S MIRROR

(Narrative, Selections, and Song)

The text of Shakespeare's plays is taken from *The Riverside Shakespeare*. Bracketed stage directions are from that text; those stage directions in parentheses are my own. K.H.B.

Dramatis Personae

FIRST PLAYER: COURT ACTOR in *Hamlet,* JAQUES in *As You Like It,* MUSICIAN in *The Merchant of Venice,* FALSTAFF in *Henry IV, Part I,* PROSPERO in *The Tempest,* LEAR in *King Lear,* MESSENGER in *Macbeth,* POLONIUS in *Hamlet,* THESEUS in *A Midsummer Night's Dream.*

SECOND PLAYER: HAMLET in *Hamlet,* MUSICIAN in *The Merchant of Venice,* CALIBAN in *The Tempest,* HOTSPUR in *Henry IV, Part I,* FERDINAND in *The Tempest,* ORLANDO in *As You Like It,* the FOOL in *King Lear,* HAMLET in *Hamlet,* PUCK in *A Midsummer Night's Dream.*

THIRD PLAYER: FIRST PLAYER in *Hamlet,* LORENZO in *The Merchant of Venice,* PRINCE HAL in *Henry IV, Part I,* PETRUCHIO in *The Taming of the Shrew,* KENT and ALBANY in *King Lear,* MACBETH in *Macbeth,* OBERON in *A Midsummer Night's Dream.*

FOURTH PLAYER: COURT ACTOR in *Hamlet,* JESSICA in *The Merchant of Venice,* JULIET in *Romeo and Juliet,* HOSTESS in *Henry IV, Part I,* MIRANDA in *The Tempest,* ROSALIND in *As You Like It,* KATHERINA in *The Taming of the Shrew,* GONERIL in *King Lear,* LADY MACBETH in *Macbeth,* TITANIA in *A Midsummer Night's Dream.*

SCENERY: *Three stools and a combination box-bench out of which properties are taken and on top of which actors may sit, stand, or walk.*

The FOUR PLAYERS *enter singing "When That I Was And A Little Tine Boy," from Shakespeare's TWELFTH NIGHT.*

FOUR PLAYERS: When that I was and a little tine boy,
With hey ho, the wind and the rain,
A foolish thing was but a toy,
For the rain it raineth every day.

But when I came to man's estate,
With hey ho, etc.
'Gainst knaves and thieves men shut their gate,
For the rain, etc.

But when I came, alas, to wive,
With hey ho, etc.
By swaggering could I never thrive,
For the rain, etc.

But when I came unto my beds,
With hey ho, etc.
With toss-pots still had drunken heads,
For the rain, etc.

A great while ago the world begun,
With hey ho, etc.
But that's all one, our play is done* (**Sing "play's begun"*)
And we'll strive to please you every day.

FIRST PLAYER: One of Shakespeare's most famous characters is Hamlet, a melancholy Danish prince whose sad duty it is to take revenge upon his uncle Claudius for the murder of his father. But Hamlet is not always sad or melancholy. A fine young Renaissance prince who loved the stage and the players, he had some advice to give to a group of actors who came to bring entertainment to his castle.

(SECOND PLAYER *addresses the others as he becomes* HAMLET *and they the* COURT ACTORS; *the* THIRD PLAYER *becomes HAMLET'S* FIRST PLAYER.)

HAMLET: Speak the speech, I pray you, as I pronounc'd it to you, trippingly on the tongue, but if you mouth it, as many of our players do, I had as live the town-crier spoke my lines. Nor do not saw the air too much with your hand, thus, but use all gently, for in the very torrent, tempest, and, as I may say, whirlwind of your passion, you must acquire and beget a temperance that may give it smoothness. O, it offends me to the soul to hear a robustious periwig-pated fellow tear a passion to totters, to very rags, to spleet the ears of the groundlings, who for the most part are capable of nothing but inexplicable dumb shows and noise. I would have such a fellow whipt for o'erdoing Termagant, it out-Herods Herod, pray you avoid it.

First Player: I warrant your honor.

Hamlet: Be not too tame neither, but let your own discretion be your tutor. Suit the action to the word, the word to the action, with this special observance, that you o'erstep not the modesty of nature: for anything so o'erdone is from the purpose of playing, whose end, both at the first and now, was and is, to hold as 'twere, the mirror up to nature: to show virtue her feature, scorn her own image, and the very age and body of the time his form and pressure. Now this overdone, or come tardy off, though it make the unskillful laugh, cannot but make the judicious grieve; the censure of which one must in your allowance o'erweigh a whole theatre of others. O, there be players that I have seen play—and heard others praise, and that highly—not to speak it profanely, that, neither having th' accent of Christians nor the gait of Christian, pagan, nor man, have so strutted and bellow'd, that I have thought some of Nature's journeymen had made men, and not made them well, they imitated humanity so abominably.

First Player: I hope we have reform'd that indifferently with us, sir.

Hamlet: O, reform it altogether. And let those that play your clowns speak no more than is set down for them, for there be of them that will themselves laugh to set on some quantity of barren spectators to laugh too, though in the mean time some necessary question of the play be then to be consider'd. That's villainous, and shows a most pitiful ambition in the fool that uses it. Go make you ready.

(*The* Four Players *disperse, dancing with the stools as they carry them to the back of the stage and speaking the following echo of* Hamlet's *speech in jazz rhythms with movements to match.*)

Four Players: Suit the action to the word, the word to the action, with this special observance, that you o'erstep not the modesty of nature: for anything so o'erdone is from the purpose of playing, whose end, both at the first and now, was and is, to hold as 'twere, the mirror up to nature. . . .

Second Player: When Hamlet says that the end of playing is to hold the mirror up to nature, he is speaking for Shakespeare. Shakespeare's plays hold the mirror up to nature as they reflect the natural world and human nature in all its richness and variety. A metaphor for life, as well as a mirror of it, Shakespeare's stage was called The Globe, and he called the globe we live on a stage. In the words of another of his characters, Jaques, in *As You Like It,* to Shakespeare all the world was a stage and all the men and women merely players.

(*The* FIRST PLAYER *becomes* JAQUES)

JAQUES: All the world's a stage,
And all the men and women merely players;
They have their exits and their entrances,
And one man in his time plays many parts,
His acts being seven ages. At first the infant,
Mewling and puking in the nurse's arms.
Then the whining schoolboy, with his satchel
And shining morning face, creeping like snail
Unwillingly to school. And then the lover,
Sighing like furnace, with a woeful ballad
Made to his mistress' eyebrow. Then a soldier,
Full of strange oaths, and bearded like the pard,
Jealous in honor, sudden, and quick in quarrel,
Seeking the bubble reputation
Even in the cannon's mouth. And then the justice,
In fair round belly with good capon lin'd,
With eyes severe and beard of formal cut,
Full of wise saws and modern instances;
And so he plays his part. The sixth age shifts
Into the lean and slipper'd pantaloon,
With spectacles on nose, and pouch on side,
His youthful hose, well sav'd, a world too wide
For his shrunk shank, and his big manly voice,
Turning again toward childish treble, pipes
And whistles in his sound. Last scene of all,
That ends this strange eventful history,
Is second childishness and mere oblivion,
Sans teeth, sans eyes, sans taste, sans every thing.

(*The* FOUR PLAYERS *echo* JAQUES' *final line:* Sans teeth, sans eyes, sans taste, sans every thing.)

FOURTH PLAYER: Often Shakespeare set the stage with words alone as we must now, asking the audience to use their imagination—to hear the scenery. Hence in *The Merchant of Venice* Lorenzo and Jessica, young lovers, create their own scene with words.

(*The* THIRD PLAYER *becomes* LORENZO *as he takes a shawl from the properties box, puts it around the* FOURTH PLAYER *who becomes* JESSICA, *and leads her stage left.*)

LORENZO: . . . How sweet the moonlight sleeps upon this bank!
Here will we sit, and let the sounds of music
Creep in our ears: soft stillness and the night
Becomes the touches of sweet harmony.
Sit, Jessica. Look how the floor of heaven
Is thick inlaid with patens of bright gold.
There's not the smallest orb which thou behold'st
But in his motion like an angel sings,
Still quiring to the young-ey'd cherubins;
Such harmony is in immortal souls,
But whilst this muddy vesture of decay
Doth grossly close it in, we cannot hear it.
Come ho, and wake Diana with a hymn,
With sweetest touches pierce your mistress' ear,
And draw her home with music.

(*The* FIRST *and* SECOND PLAYERS *serenade the lovers.*)

FOURTH PLAYER: The sweet sounds of nature are created too by Caliban, a misshapen monster in *The Tempest,* who despite his villainy and deformity responds to the beauties of nature on the desert island on which he dwells.

(*The* SECOND PLAYER *removes a cloak from the box-bench and becomes* CALIBAN.)

CALIBAN: Be not afeard, the isle is full of noises,
Sounds, and sweet airs, that give delight, and hurt not.
Sometimes a thousand twangling instruments
Will hum about mine ears; and sometime voices,
That if I then had wak'd after long sleep,
Will make me sleep again, and then in dreaming,
The clouds methought would open, and show riches
Ready to drop upon me, that when I wak'd,
I cried to dream again.

(*The* FOUR PLAYERS *echo* CALIBAN, *repeating the word* Dream *as they move in slow motion to their positions for the next selection.*)

THIRD PLAYER: In *Romeo and Juliet,* the lovely Juliet is in despair because her father has ordered her to marry Paris. Juliet is already married to Romeo, though secretly because of the enmity between their parents, and now Romeo is banished for killing one of Juliet's kinsmen. Friar Lawrence, who has married the young couple, would help Juliet evade the marriage planned by her father and encourages her to take a sleeping potion which will give her the appearance of death. Once she is buried in the family vault, the Friar will bring Romeo to her side, she will wake up, and the lovers will be united. About to drink the potion, Juliet paints in her imagination the fearful place where she will awaken.

(*The* FOURTH PLAYER *becomes* JULIET.)

JULIET: I have a faint cold fear thrills through my veins,
That almost freezes up the heat of life.
I'll call them back again to comfort me.
Nurse!—What should she do here?
My dismal scene I needs must act alone.
Come, vial.
What if this mixture do not work at all?
Shall I be married then to-morrow morning?
No, no, this shall forbid it. Lie thou there.

[*Laying down her dagger.*]

What if it be a poison which the friar
Subtilly hath minist'red to have me dead,
Lest in this marriage he should be dishonor'd
Because he married me before to Romeo?
I fear it is, and yet methinks it should not,
For he hath still been tried a holy man.
How if, when I am laid into the tomb,
I wake before the time that Romeo
Come to redeem me? there's a fearful point!
Shall I not then be stifled in the vault,
To whose foul mouth no healthsome air breathes in,
And there die strangled ere my Romeo comes?
Or if I live, is it not very like
The horrible conceit of death and night,

Together with the terror of the place—
As in a vault, an ancient receptacle,
Where for this many hundred years the bones
Of all my buried ancestors are pack'd,
Where bloody Tybalt, yet but green in earth,
Lies festering in his shroud, where, as they say,
At some hours in the night spirits resort—
Alack, alack, is it not like that I,
So early waking—what with loathsome smells,
And shrikes like mandrakes' torn out of the earth,
That living mortals hearing them, run mad—
O, if I wake, shall I not be distraught,
Environed with all these hideous fears?
And madly play with my forefathers' joints,
And pluck the mangled Tybalt from his shroud,
And, in this rage, with some great kinsman's bone,
As with a club, dash out my desp'rate brains?
O, look! methinks I see my cousin's ghost
Seeking out Romeo, that did spit his body
Upon a rapier's point: stay, Tybalt, stay!
Romeo, Romeo, Romeo! Here's drink—I drink to thee.

THIRD PLAYER: And so the stage is set, for love, for dreams, for death. But what of the players? If the end of playing is to hold the mirror up to nature, to show "virtue her feature, scorn her own image, and the very age and body of the time his form and pressure," what better way than to turn to English history, to see what could be reflected of the present in the past. Prince Hal, the heir to the English throne in *Henry IV: Part I,* is a young lad whose father, Henry IV, despairs of him because he spends so much time in tavern life with a great, fat, roguish knight, Sir John Falstaff. The king would rather have Hal be as brave as the romantic Hotspur, the king's enemy, a man who would dare all for the sake of honor.

(SECOND PLAYER *becomes* HOTSPUR, FIRST PLAYER FALSTAFF, THIRD PLAYER THE PRINCE, *and the* FOURTH PLAYER THE HOSTESS.)

HOTSPUR: By heaven, methinks it were an easy leap,
To pluck bright honor from the pale-fac'd moon,
Or dive into the bottom of the deep,
Where fadom-line could never touch the ground,

And pluck up drowned honor by the locks,
So he that doth redeem her thence might wear
Without corrival all her dignities;
But out upon this half-fac'd fellowship!

THIRD PLAYER: Falstaff, Hal's friend and, in a sense, his teacher, doubts if honor is as valuable as all that and is frightened when on the battlefield.

FALSTAFF: Hal, if thou see me down in the battle and bestride me, so; 'tis a point of friendship.

PRINCE: Nothing but a Colossus can do thee that friendship. Say thy prayers, and farewell.

FALSTAFF: I would 'twere bed-time, Hal, and all well.

PRINCE: Why, thou owest God a death.

(THIRD PLAYER *as* PRINCE *turns out of the scene.* FALSTAFF *enters the audience to share his rhetorical questions with them.*)

FALSTAFF: 'Tis not due yet, I would be loath to pay him before his day. What need I be so forward with him that calls not on me? Well, 'tis no matter, honor pricks me on. Yea, but how if honor prick me off when I come on? how then? Can honor set to a leg? No. Or an arm? No. Or take away the grief of a wound? No. Honor hath no skill in surgery then? No. What is honor? A word. What is in that word honor? what is that honor? Air. A trim reckoning! Who hath it? He that died a' Wednesday. Doth he feel it? No. Doth he hear it? No. 'Tis insensible, then? Yea, to the dead. But will't not live with the living? No. Why? Detraction will not suffer it. Therefore I'll none of it, honor is a mere scutcheon. And so ends my catechism.

THIRD PLAYER: Hal comes to an idea of honor somewhere between that of the romantic Hotspur and the realistic, down-to-earth Falstaff. He knows that the time will come when he must part from his fat cowardly friend if he is to assume his responsibilities as prince and then king, but he will never part with the lessons he has learned from Falstaff about life. In jest, Hal and Falstaff make up a play about the time when Hal will be summoned to appear before the king.

(The actors take their places for the following tavern scene singing the drinking song from OTHELLO. They remove beer mugs, dagger, and cushion from the box-bench.)

FOUR PLAYERS: And let me the canakin clink, clink;
And let me the canakin clink.
A soldier's a man;
O, man's life's but a span;
Why then let a soldier drink.

PRINCE: Do thou stand for my father and examine me upon the particulars of my life.

FALSTAFF: Shall I? Content. This chair shall be my state, this dagger my sceptre, and this cushion my crown.

PRINCE: Thy state is taken for a join'd-stool, thy golden sceptre for a leaden dagger, and thy precious rich crown for a pitiful bald crown!

FALSTAFF: Well, an the fire of grace be not quite out of thee, now shalt thou be mov'd. Give me a cup of sack to make my eyes look red, that it may be thought I have wept, for I must speak in passion, and I will do it in King Cambyses' vein.

PRINCE: Well, here is my leg.

FALSTAFF: And here is my speech. Stand aside, nobility.

HOSTESS: O Jesu, this is excellent sport, i' faith!

FALSTAFF: Weep not, sweet queen; for trickling tears are vain.

HOSTESS: O, the father, how he holds his countenance!

FALSTAFF: For God's sake, lords, convey my tristful queen,
For tears do stop the floodgates of her eyes.

HOSTESS: O Jesu, he doth it as like one of these harlotry players as ever I see!

FALSTAFF: Peace, good pint-pot; peace, good ticklebrain. Harry, I not only marvel where thou spendest thy time, but also how thou art accompanied; for though the camomile, the more it is trodden on, the faster it grows, yet youth, the more it is wasted, the sooner it wears. That thou art my son I have partly thy mother's word, partly my own opinion, but chiefly a villainous trick of thine eye, and a foolish hanging of thy nether lip, that doth warrant me. If then thou be son to me, here lies the point: why, being son to me, art thou so pointed at? Shall the blessed sun of heaven prove a micher and eat blackberries? a question not to be asked. Shall the son of England prove a thief and take purses? a question to be ask'd. There is a thing, Harry, which thou hast often heard of, and it is known to many in our land by the name of pitch. This pitch (as ancient writers do report) doth defile, so doth the company thou keepest; for, Harry, now I do not speak to thee in drink, but in tears; not in pleasure, but in passion; not in words only, but in woes also. And yet there is a virtuous man whom I have often noted in thy company, but I know not his name.

PRINCE: What manner of man, an it like your majesty?

FALSTAFF: A goodly portly man, i' faith, and a corpulent, of a cheerful look, a pleasing eye, and a most noble carriage, and as I think, his age some fifty, or, by'r lady, inclining to three score; and now I remember me, his name is Falstaff. If that man should be lewdly given, he deceiveth me; for Harry, I see virtue in his looks. If then the tree may be known by the fruit, as the fruit by the tree, then, peremptorily I speak it, there is virtue in that Falstaff; him keep with, the rest banish. And tell me now, thou naughty varlet, tell me, where hast thou been this month?

PRINCE: Dost thou speak like a king? Do thou stand for me, and I'll play my father.

FALSTAFF: Depose me? if thou dost it half so gravely, so majestically, both in word and matter, hang me up by the heels for a rabbit-sucker or a poulter's hare.

PRINCE: Well, here I am set.

FALSTAFF: And here I stand. Judge, my masters.

PRINCE: Now, Harry, whence come you?

FALSTAFF: My noble lord, from Eastcheap.

PRINCE: The complaints I hear of thee are grievous.

FALSTAFF: 'Sblood, my lord, they are false. Nay, I'll tickle ye for a young prince, i' faith.

PRINCE: Swearest thou, ungracious boy? hence-forth ne'er look on me. Thou art violently carried away from grace, there is a devil haunts thee in the likeness of an old fat man, a tun of man is thy companion. Why dost thou converse with that trunk of humours, that bolting-hutch of beastliness, that swoll'n parcel of dropsies, that huge bombard of sack, that stuff'd cloak-bag of guts, that roasted Manningtree ox with the pudding in his belly, that reverend Vice, that grey Iniquity, that father ruffian, that vanity in years? Wherein is he good, but to taste sack and drink it? wherein neat and cleanly, but to carve a capon and eat it? wherein cunning, but in craft? wherein crafty, but in villainy? wherein villainous, but in all things? wherein worthy, but in nothing?

FALSTAFF: I would your Grace would take me with you. Whom means your Grace?

PRINCE: That villainous abominable misleader of youth, Falstaff, that old white-bearded Sathan.

FALSTAFF: My lord, the man I know.

PRINCE: I know thou dost.

FALSTAFF: But to say I know more harm in him than in myself, were to say more than I know. That he is old, the more the pity, his white hairs do witness it, but that he is, saving your reverence, a whoremaster, that I utterly deny. If sack and sugar be a fault, God help the wicked! if to be old and merry be a sin, then many an old host that I know is damn'd. If to be fat be to be hated, then Pharaoh's lean kine are to be lov'd. No, my good lord, banish Peto, banish Bardolph, banish Poins, but for sweet Jack Falstaff, kind Jack Falstaff, true Jack Falstaff, valiant Jack Falstaff, and therefore more valiant, being, as he is old Jack Falstaff, banish not him thy Harry's company, banish not him thy Harry's company—banish plump Jack, and banish all the world.

PRINCE: I do, I will.

THIRD PLAYER: And in a later play, sad though it was, he did.

FIRST PLAYER: Shakespeare wrote, then, of honor, of history, and of the education of a prince. But as he held the mirror up to nature he often turned as well to that very well known passion which comes to us all sooner or later—love. In *The Tempest,* Miranda has been stranded on a desert island with her father since her infancy. She has only seen her father and Caliban, the beast-like creature who serves her father, but no other man. Now Ferdinand, a young prince swept onto her island by the roaring tempest her magician father has created, seems the most beautiful being she has ever seen and the young couple fall in love at first sight. Prospero, Miranda's father, is wary of the young man's intentions and sets him the task of carrying logs as a test.

(*The* SECOND PLAYER *carries the stools as logs as he becomes the love-struck* FERDINAND; *the* FOURTH PLAYER *becomes* MIRANDA, *the* FIRST PLAYER, PROSPERO.)

FERDINAND: There be some sports are painful, and their labor
Delight in them sets off; some kinds of baseness
Are nobly undergone; and most poor matters
Point to rich ends. This my mean task
Would be as heavy to me as odious, but
The mistress which I serve quickens what's dead,
And makes my labors pleasures. O, she is
Ten times more gentle than her father's crabbed;
And he's compos'd of harshness. I must remove
Some thousands of these logs, and pile them up,
Upon a sore injunction. My sweet mistress
Weeps when she sees me work, and says, such baseness
Had never like executor. I forget;
But these sweet thoughts do even refresh my labors,
Most busil'est when I do it.
MIRANDA: Alas, now pray you
Work not so hard. I would the lightning had
Burnt up those logs that you are enjoin'd to pile!
Pray set it down, and rest you. When this burns,
'Twill weep for having wearied you. My father
Is hard at study; pray now rest yourself,
He's safe for these three hours.
FERDINAND: O most dear mistress,
The sun will set before I shall discharge
What I must strive to do.
MIRANDA: If you'll sit down,
I'll bear your logs the while. Pray give me that,
I'll carry it to the pile.
FERDINAND: No, precious creature,
I had rather crack my sinews, break my back,
Than you should such dishonour undergo,
While I sit lazy by.
MIRANDA: It would become me
As well as it does you; and I should do it
With much more ease, for my good will is to it,
And yours it is against.
PROSPERO: [*Aside.*] Poor worm, thou art infected!
This visitation shows it.
MIRANDA: You look wearily.

FERDINAND: No, noble mistress; 'tis fresh morning with me
When you are by at night. I do beseech you—
Chiefly that I might set it in my prayers—
What is your name?
MIRANDA: Miranda.—O my father,
I have broke your hest to say so.
FERDINAND: Admired Miranda,
Indeed the top of admiration! worth
What's dearest to the world! Full many a lady
I have ey'd with best regard, and many a time
Th' harmony of their tongues hath into bondage
Brought my too diligent ear. For several virtues
Have I lik'd several women, never any
With so full soul, but some defect in her
Did quarrel with the noblest grace she ow'd,
And put it to the foil. But you, O you,
So perfect and so peerless, are created
Of every creature's best!
MIRANDA: I do not know
One of my sex; no woman's face remember,
Save, from my glass, mine own; nor have I seen
More that I may call men than you, good friend,
And my dear father. How features are abroad
I am skilless of; but, by my modesty
(The jewell in my dower), I would not wish
Any companion in the world but you;
Nor can imagination form a shape,
Besides yourself, to like of. But I prattle
Something too wildly, and my father's precepts
I therein do forget.
FERDINAND: I am, in my condition,
A prince, Miranda; I do think, a king
(I would, not so!), and would no more endure
This wooden slavery than to suffer
The flesh-fly blow my mouth. Hear my soul speak:
The very instant that I saw you, did
My heart fly to your service, there resides,
To make me slave to it, and for your sake
Am I this patient log-man.

MIRANDA: Do you love me?
FERDINAND: O heaven, O earth, bear witness to this sound,
And crown what I profess with kind event
If I speak true! if hollowly, invert
What best is boded me to mischief! I,
Beyond all limit of what else i' the world,
Do love, prize, honor you.
MIRANDA: I am a fool
To weep at what I am glad of.
PROSPERO: [*Aside.*] Fair encounter
Of two most rare affections! Heavens rain grace
On that which breeds between 'em!
FERDINAND: Wherefore weep you?
MIRANDA: At mine unworthiness, that dare not offer
What I desire to give; and much less take
What I shall die to want. But this is trifling,
And all the more it seeks to hide itself,
The bigger bulk it shows. Hence, bashful cunning,
And prompt me, plain and holy innocence!
I am your wife, if you will marry me;
If not, I'll die your maid. To be your fellow
You may deny me, but I'll be your servant,
Whether you will or no.
FERDINAND: My mistress, dearest,
And I thus humble ever.
MIRANDA: My husband then?
FERDINAND: Ay, with a heart as willing
As bondage e'er of freedom. Here's my hand.
MIRANDA: And mine, with my heart in't. And now farewell
Till half an hour hence.
FERDINAND: A thousand, thousand!
PROSPERO: So glad of this as they I cannot be,
Who are surpris'd withal; but my rejoicing
At nothing can be more. I'll to my book,
For yet ere supper-time must I perform
Much business appertaining.

FIRST PLAYER: Othello, in Shakespeare's tragedy of that name, is a distinguished Moor, a black man, a brave and competent soldier whose conduct in the Venetian wars against the Turks has raised him to the rank of general. He has secretly married the fair Desdemona and now describes the romantic wooing of the lovely girl to the questioning Duke and the angry father.

(SECOND PLAYER *becomes* OTHELLO, PLAYERS ONE *and* THREE *the questioning* DUKE *and the angry* FATHER.)

OTHELLO: Her father lov'd me, oft invited me;
Still question'd me the story of my life
From year to year—the battles, sieges, fortunes,
That I have pass'd.
I ran it through, even from my boyish days
To th' very moment that he bade me tell it;
Wherein I spoke of most disastrous chances:
Of moving accidents by flood and field,
Of hair-breadth scapes i' th' imminent deadly breach,
Of being taken by the insolent foe
And sold to slavery, of my redemption thence
And portance in my travel's history;
Wherein of antres vast and deserts idle,
Rough quarries, rocks, and hills whose heads touch heaven,
It was my hint to speak—such was the process—
And of the Cannibals that each other eat,
The Anthropophagi, and men whose heads
Do grow beneath their shoulders. These things to hear
Would Desdemona seriously incline;
But still the house affairs would draw her thence
Which ever as she could with haste dispatch,
She'ld come again, and with a greedy ear
Devour up my discourse. Which I observing,
Took once a pliant hour, and found good means
To draw from her a prayer of earnest heart
That I would all my pilgrimage dilate,
Whereof by parcels she had something heard,
But not intentively. I did consent,
And often did beguile her of her tears,
When I did speak of some distressful stroke
That my youth suffer'd. My story being done
She gave me for my pains a world of sighs;
She swore, in faith 'twas strange, 'twas passing strange;
'Twas pitiful, 'twas wondrous pitiful.

She wish'd she had not heard it, yet she wish'd
That heaven had made her such a man. She thank'd me,
And bade me, if I had a friend that lov'd her,
I should but teach him how to tell my story,
And that would woo her. Upon this hint I spake:
She lov'd me for the dangers I had pass'd,
And I lov'd her that she did pity them.
This only is the witchcraft I have used.

FIRST PLAYER: In Shakespeare's comedy, *As You Like It,* Rosalind loves Orlando and Orlando loves Rosalind. Orlando has fled the Duke's wrath and roams the forest of Arden writing poems of his love which he attaches to trees. Rosalind, forced as well to flee the court, roams the forest dressed for protection as a boy. In the following scene between the young people, Rosalind does not reveal her identity to Orlando but decides to test his love.

The FOURTH PLAYER *removes a boy's cap from the box-bench as she becomes* ROSALIND *imitating a boy, while the* SECOND PLAYER *becomes* ORLANDO. *Two stools serve as tree trunks on which they sit.)*

ORLANDO: Where dwell you, pretty youth?

ROSALIND: With this shepherdess, my sister; here in the skirts of the forest, like fringe upon a petticoat.

ORLANDO: Are you native of this place?

ROSALIND: As the cony that you see dwell where she is kindled.

ORLANDO: Your accent is something finer than you could purchase in so remov'd a dwelling.

ROSALIND: I have been told so of many; but indeed an old religious uncle of mine taught me to speak, who was in his youth an inland man, one that knew courtship too well, for there he fell in love. I have heard him read many lectures against it, and I thank God I am not a woman, to be touch'd with so many giddy offences as he hath generally tax'd their whole sex withal.

ORLANDO: Can you remember any of the principal evils that he laid to the charge of women?

ROSALIND: There were none principal, they were all like one another as halfpence are, every one fault seeming monstrous till his fellow-fault came to match it.

ORLANDO: I prithee recount some of them.

ROSALIND: No; I will not cast away my physic but on those that are sick. There is a man haunts the forest, that abuses our young plants with carving "Rosalind" on their barks; hangs odes upon hawthorns, and elegies on brambles; all, forsooth, deifying the name of Rosalind. If I could meet that fancy-monger, I would give him some good counsel, for he seems to have the quotidian of love upon him.

ORLANDO: I am he that is so love-shak'd, I pray you, tell me your remedy.

ROSALIND: There is none of my uncle's marks upon you. He taught me how to know a man in love; in which cage of rushes I am sure you are not prisoner.

ORLANDO: What were his marks?

ROSALIND: A lean cheek, which you have not; a blue eye and sunken, which you have not; an unquestionable spirit, which you have not; a beard neglected, which you have not (but I pardon you for that, for simply your having in beard is a younger brother's revenue); then your hose should be ungarter'd, your bonnet unbanded, your sleeve unbutton'd, your shoe untied, and every thing about you demonstrating a careless desolation. But you are no such man; you are rather point-device in your accoutrements, as loving yourself, than seeming the lover of any other.

ORLANDO: Fair youth, I would I could make thee believe I love.

ROSALIND: Me believe it? You may as soon make her that you love believe it, which, I warrant she is apter to do than to confess she does. That is one of the points in the which women still give the lie to their consciences. But in good sooth, are you he that hangs the verses on the trees, wherein Rosalind is so admir'd?

ORLANDO: I swear to thee, youth, by the white hand of Rosalind, I am that he, that unfortunate he.

ROSALIND: But are you so much in love as your rhymes speak?

ORLANDO: Neither rhyme nor reason can express how much.

ROSALIND: Love is merely a madness, and I tell you, deserves as well a dark house and a whip as madmen do; and the reason why they are not so punish'd and cur'd is, that the lunacy is so ordinary that the whippers are in love too. Yet I profess curing it by counsel.

ORLANDO: Did you ever cure any so?

ROSALIND: Yes, one, and in this manner. He was to imagine me his love, his mistress; and I set him every day to woo me. At which time would I, being but a moonish youth, grieve, be effeminate, changeable, longing and liking, proud, fantastical, apish, shallow, inconstant, full of tears, full of smiles; for every passion something, and for no passion truly any thing, as boys and women are for the most part cattle of this color; would now like him, now loathe him; then entertain him, then forswear him; now weep for him, then spit at him; that I drave my suitor from his mad humour of love to a living humour of madness, which was, to forswear the full stream of the world, and to live in a nook merely monastic. And thus I cured him, and this way will I take upon me to wash your liver as clean as a sound sheep's heart, that there shall not be one spot of love in't.

ORLANDO: I would not be cur'd, youth.

ROSALIND: I would cure you, if you would but call me Rosalind, and come every day to my cote and woo me.

ORLANDO: Now, by the faith of my love, I will. Tell me where it is.

ROSALIND: Go with me to it, and I'll show it you; and by the way, you shall tell me where in the forest you live. Will you go?

ORLANDO: With all my heart, good youth.

ROSALIND: Nay, you must call me Rosalind.

FIRST PLAYER: If Rosalind wishes to test Orlando's love, Petruchio in *The Taming of the Shrew,* a man who has come to Padua to find a rich wife, decides to try his luck at taming the shrewish, bad tempered Katherina, a woman who will have nothing to do with love. And so the battle of the sexes rages as they meet.

(THIRD PLAYER *becomes* PETRUCHIO, *the* FOURTH PLAYER, KATHERINA.)

PETRUCHIO: I'll attend her here,
And woo her with some spirit when she comes.
Say that she rail, why then I'll tell her plain
She sings as sweetly as a nightingale;
Say that she frown, I'll say she looks as clear

As morning roses newly wash'd with dew;
Say she be mute, and will not speak a word,
Then I'll commend her volubility,
And say she uttereth piercing eloquence;
If she do bid me pack, I'll give her thanks,
As though she bid me stay by her a week;
If she deny to wed, I'll crave the day
When I shall ask the banes, and when be married.
But here she comes, and now, Petruchio, speak.
Good morrow, Kate, for that's your name, I hear.

KATHERINA: Well have you heard, but something hard of hearing:
They call me Katherine that do talk of me.

PETRUCHIO: You lie, in faith, for you are call'd plain Kate,
And bonny Kate, and sometimes Kate the curst;
But Kate, the prettiest Kate in Christendom,
Kate of Kate-Hall, my super-dainty Kate,
For dainties are all Kates, and therefore, Kate,
Take this of me, Kate of my consolation—
Hearing thy mildness prais'd in every town,
Thy virtues spoke of, and thy beauty sounded,
Yet not so deeply as to thee belongs,
Myself am mov'd to woo thee for my wife.

(He kneels before her, taking her hand.)

KATHERINA: Mov'd! In good time! Let him that mov'd you hither
Remove you hence. I knew you at the first
You were a moveable.

(She pushes him over.)

PETRUCHIO: Why, what's a moveable?
KATHERINA: A join'd-stool.
PETRUCHIO: Thou has hit it: come sit on me.

(He pulls her onto one knee.)

KATHERINA: Asses are made to bear, and so are you.
PETRUCHIO: Women are made to bear and so are you.
KATHERINA: No such jade as you, if me you mean.
PETRUCHIO: Alas, good Kate, I will not burden thee,
For knowing thee to be but young and light.

KATHERINA: Too light for such a swain as you to catch,
And yet as heavy as my weight should be.

(They have been struggling, and she succeeds in pushing him over.)

PETRUCHIO: Should be! should—buzz!
KATHERINA: Well ta'en, and like a buzzard.

(He is crawling and she grabs his nose.)

PETRUCHIO: O slow-wing'd turtle, shall a buzzard take thee?
KATHERINA: Ay, for a turtle, as he takes a buzzard.
PETRUCHIO: Come, come, you wasp, i' faith you are too angry.

(Rising, he grabs her.)

KATHERINA: If I be waspish, best beware my sting.
PETRUCHIO: My remedy is then to pluck it out.
KATHERINA: Ay, if the fool could find it where it lies.
PETRUCHIO: Who knows not where a wasp does wear his sting?
In his tail.

(He pinches her rear.)

KATHERINA: In his tongue.
PETRUCHIO: Whose tongue?
KATHERINA: Yours, if you talk of tails, and so farewell.
PETRUCHIO: What, with my tongue in your tail? Nay, come again,
Good Kate; I am a gentleman.
KATHERINA: That I'll try.

[*She strikes him*]

PETRUCHIO: I swear I'll cuff you, if you strike again.
KATHERINA: So may you lose your arms.
If you strike me, you are no gentleman,
And if no gentleman, why then no arms.
PETRUCHIO: A herald, Kate? O, put me in thy books!
KATHERINA: What is your crest? a coxcomb?
PETRUCHIO: A combless cock, so Kate will be my hen.
KATHERINA: No cock of mine, you crow too like a craven.
PETRUCHIO: Nay, come, Kate, come; you must not look so sour.
KATHERINA: It is my fashion, when I see a crab.
PETRUCHIO: Why, here's no crab; and therefore look not sour.
KATHERINA: There is, there is.
PETRUCHIO: Then show it me.

KATHERINA: Had I a glass, I would.
PETRUCHIO: What, you mean my face?
KATHERINA: Well aim'd of such a young one.
PETRUCHIO: Now, by Saint George, I am too young for you.
KATHERINA: Yet you are wither'd.
PETRUCHIO: 'Tis with cares.
KATHERINA: I care not.
PETRUCHIO: Nay, hear you, Kate. In sooth you scape not so.
KATHERINA: I chafe you if I tarry. Let me go.

(He pulls her to box-bench and down over his knees.)

PETRUCHIO: No, not a whit, I find you passing gentle:
'Twas told me you were rough and coy and sullen,
And now I find report a very liar;
For thou are pleasant, gamesome, passing courteous,
But slow in speech, yet sweet as spring-time flowers.
Thou canst not frown, thou canst not look askaunce,
Nor bite the lip, as angry wenches will,
Nor hast thou pleasure to be cross in talk;
But thou with mildness entertain'st thy wooers,
With gentle conference, soft, and affable.

(She bites him, frees herself, and having lost a shoe in the tussle, limps away.)

Why does the world report that Kate doth limp?
O sland'rous world! Kate like the hazel-twig
Is straight and slender, and as brown in hue
As hazel-nuts, and sweeter than the kernels.
O, let me see thee walk. Thou dost not halt.
KATHERINA: Go, fool, and whom thou keep'st command.

(He jumps on the box-bench.)

PETRUCHIO: Did ever Dian so become a grove
As Kate this chamber with her princely gait?
O, be thou Dian, and let her be Kate.
And then let Kate be chaste, and Dian sportful!
KATHERINA: Where did you study all this goodly speech?
PETRUCHIO: It is extempore, from my mother-wit.
KATHERINA: A witty mother! witless else her son.
PETRUCHIO: Am I not wise?
KATHERINA: Yes, keep you warm.

(He jumps down and grabs her, places her on the box, and, despite her struggles, puts her shoe back on.)

PETRUCHIO: Marry, so I mean, sweet Katherine, in thy bed;
And therefore setting all this chat aside,
Thus in plain terms: your father hath consented
That you shall be my wife; your dowry 'greed on;
And will you, nill you, I will marry you.
Now, Kate, I am a husband for your turn,
For by this light whereby I see thy beauty,
Thy beauty that doth make me like thee well,
Thou must be married to no man but me;
For I am he am born to tame you, Kate,
And bring you from a wild Kate to a Kate
Conformable as other household Kates.

(Standing behind her, he holds her arm behind her and swings her up and back to him.)

Here comes your father. Never make denial;
I must and will have Katherine to my wife.

SECOND PLAYER: Ferdinand gets his Miranda *(He kisses* FOURTH PLAYER *on one cheek)* Orlando gets his Rosalind *(He kisses the* FOURTH PLAYER *on the other cheek)* and Petruchio gets his Katherine (PETRUCHIO *swirls* FOURTH PLAYER *into a dip),* though perhaps he is to be pitied.

FIRST PLAYER: And we all get a brief intermission.

(The FOUR PLAYERS *exit singing the opening song,* "When I Was And A Little Tine Boy.")

PART II

SCENE: The FOUR PLAYERS *enter again singing* "When That I Was And A Little Tine Boy." *They re-enact the ending of Part I with the same motions.*

SECOND PLAYER: Ferdinand gets his Miranda, Orlando gets his Rosalind, and Petruchio gets his Katherine, though perhaps he is still to be pitied. The lovers do not all live happily ever after, however, for Shakespeare's mirror is true to life and reflects its tragic as well as its romantic and comic moments.

Othello, who wooed and won the fair Desdemona, is worked up into such wild jealousy by the evil Iago that he kills his innocent bride, and upon discovering her innocence, himself. King Lear is another great tragic character who listens to the wrong people, misunderstands the nature of love and himself, and suffers far more than his actions merit. King of Britain, over which he has ruled for many years, Lear decides to retire and divide his lands among his three daughters, whom he will live with by turns. Because Cordelia cannot express her love as lavishly as her sisters, Goneril and Regan, she is disinherited by her father. But the king's Fool, a court jester, knows that Lear has chosen to trust the evil sisters, not the good, and he chides the mistaken Lear for his actions and his blindness.

(FIRST PLAYER *becomes* LEAR, SECOND PLAYER *the* FOOL, THIRD PLAYER KENT, *and then* ALBANY, *the* FOURTH PLAYER GONERIL.)

LEAR: How, now, my pretty knave, how dost thou?

FOOL: Sirrah, you were best take my coxcomb.

KENT: Why, Fool?

FOOL: Why? for taking one's part that's out of favor. Nay, and thou canst not smile as the wind sits, thou'lt catch cold shortly. There, take my coxcomb. Why, this fellow hath banish'd two on's daughters, and did the third a blessing against his will; if thou follow him, thou must needs wear my coxcomb.—How now, nuncle? Would I had two coxcombs and two daughters!

LEAR: Why, my boy?

FOOL: If I gave them all my living, I'ld keep my coxcombs myself. There's mine, beg another of thy daughters.

LEAR: Take heed, sirrah—the whip.

FOOL: Truth's a dog must to kennel; he must be whipt out, when the Lady Brach may stand by th' fire and stink.

LEAR: A pestilent gall to me!

FOOL: Sirrah, I'll teach thee a speech.

LEAR: Do.

FOOL: Mark it, nuncle:

Have more than thou showest,
Speak less than thou knowest,
Lend less than thou owest,

Ride more than thou goest,
Learn more than thou trowest,
Set less than thou throwest;
Leave thy drink and thy whore,
And keep in a' door,
And thou shalt have more
Than two tens to a score.

KENT: This is nothing, Fool.

FOOL: Then 'tis like the breath of an unfee'd lawyer, you gave me nothing for 't. Can you make no use of nothing, nuncle?

LEAR: Why, no, boy, nothing can be made out of nothing.

FOOL: [*to* KENT] Prithee, tell him, so much the rent of his land comes to. He will not believe a fool.

LEAR: A bitter fool!

FOOL: Dost thou know the difference, my boy, between a bitter fool and a sweet one?

LEAR: No, lad, teach me.

FOOL: That lord that counsell'd thee
To give away thy land,
Come place him here by me;
Do thou for him stand:
The sweet and bitter fool
Will presently appear:
The one in motley here,
The other found out there.

LEAR: Dost thou call me, fool, boy?

FOOL: All thy other titles thou hast given away, that thou was born with.

KENT: This is not altogether fool, my lord.

FOOL: No, faith, lords and great men will not let me; if I had a monopoly out, they would have part an't. And ladies too, they will not let me have all the fool to myself, they'll be snatching. Nuncle, give me an egg, and I'll give thee two crowns.

LEAR: What two crowns shall they be?

FOOL: Why, after I have cut the egg i' th' middle and eat up the meat, the two crowns of the egg. When thou clovest thy crown i' th' middle and gav'st away both parts, thou bor'st thine ass on thy back o'er the dirt. Thou hadst little wit in thy bald crown when thy gav'st thy golden one away.

If I speak like myself in this, let him be whipped that first finds it so.
[*Sings*] Fools had ne'er less grace in a year,
For wise men are grown foppish,
And know not how their wits to wear,
Their manners are so apish.

LEAR: When were you wont to be so full of songs, sirrah?

FOOL: I have used it, nuncle, e'er since thou mad'st thy daughters thy mothers, for when thou gav'st them the rod, and putt'st down thine own breeches,
[*Sings*] Then they for sudden joy did weep,
And I for sorrow sung,
That such a king should play bo-peep,
And go the fools among.
Prithee, nuncle, keep a schoolmaster that can
teach thy Fool to lie—I would fain learn to lie.

LEAR: An you lie, sirrah, we'll have you whipt.

FOOL: I marvel what kin thou and thy daughters are: they'll have me whipt for speaking true; thou'lt have me whipt for lying; and sometimes I am whipt for holding my peace. I had rather be any kind o' thing than a Fool, and yet I would not be thee, nuncle: thou hast par'd thy wit o' both sides, and left nothing i' th' middle. Here comes one o' the parings.

[*Enter* GONERIL]

LEAR: How now, daughter? what makes that frontlet on? You are too much of late i' th' frown.

FOOL: Thou wast a pretty fellow when thou hadst no need to care for her frowning; now thou art an 0 without a figure. I am better than thou art now, I am a Fool, thou art nothing. [*to* GONERIL] Yes, forsooth, I will hold my tongue; so your face bids me, though you say nothing.
Mum, mum:
He that keeps nor crust nor crumb,
Weary of all, shall want some.
[*pointing to* LEAR] That's a sheal'd peascod.

GONERIL: Not only, sir, this your all-licens'd Fool,
But other of your insolent retinue
Do hourly carp and quarrel, breaking forth
In rank and not-to-be endur'd riots. Sir,
I had thought, by making this well known unto you,

To have found a safe redress, but now grow fearful,
By what yourself too late have spoke and done,
That you protect this course and put it on
By your allowance; which if you should, the fault
Would not scape censure, nor the redresses sleep,
Which, in the tender of a wholesome weal,
Might in their working do you that offence,
Which else were shame, that then necessity
Will call discreet proceeding.
Fool: For, you know, nuncle,
The hedge-sparrow fed the cuckoo so long,
That it had it head bit off by it young.
So out went the candle, and we were left darkling.
Lear: Are you our daughter?
Goneril: I would you would make use of your good wisdom
(Whereof I know you are fraught) and put away
These dispositions that of late transport you
From what you rightly are.
Fool: May not an ass know when the cart draws the horse?
[*Sings*] Whoop, Jug! I love thee.
Lear: Does any here know me? This is not Lear.
Does Lear walk thus? speak thus? Where are his eyes?
Either his notion weakens, his discernings
Are lethargied—Ha! waking? 'Tis not so.
Who is it that can tell me who I am?
Fool: Lear's shadow.
Lear: I would learn that, for by the marks of sovereignty,
Knowledge and reason, I should be false persuaded
I had daughters.
Fool: Which they will make an obedient father.
Lear: Your name, fair gentlewoman?
Goneril: This admiration, sir, is much o' the savor
Of other your new pranks. I do beseech you
To understand my purposes aright,
As you are old and reverend, you should be wise.
Here do you keep a hundred knights and squires,
Men so disorder'd, so debosh'd and bold,
That this our court, infected with their manners,
Shows like a riotous inn. Epicurism and lust
Make it more like a tavern or a brothel

Than a grac'd palace. The shame itself doth speak
For instant remedy. Be then desir'd
By her, that else will take the thing she begs,
A little to disquantity your train,
And the remainders that shall still depend,
To be such men as may besort your age,
Which know themselves and you.

LEAR: Darkness and devils!
Saddle my horses; call my train together!
Degenerate bastard, I'll not trouble thee;
Yet have I left a daughter.

GONERIL: You strike my people,
And your disorder'd rabble make servants of their betters.

[*Enter* ALBANY]

LEAR: Woe, that too late repents!—O, sir, are you come?
Is it your will? Speak, sir.—Prepare my horses.—
Ingratitude! thou marble-hearted fiend,
More hideous when thou show'st thee in a child
Than the sea-monster.

ALBANY: Pray, sir, be patient.

LEAR: [*to* GONERIL] Detested kite, thou liest.
My train are men of choice and rarest parts,
That all particulars of duty know,
And in the most exact regard support
The worships of their name. O most small fault,
How ugly didst thou in Cordelia show!
Which, like an engine, wrench'd my frame of nature
From the fix'd place; drew from my heart all love,
And added to the gall. O Lear, Lear, Lear!
Beat at this gate, that let thy folly in

[*striking his head*]

And thy dear judgment out! Go, go, my people.

ALBANY: My lord, I am guiltless as I am ignorant
Of what hath moved you.

LEAR: It may be so, my lord.

(He locates NATURE *in the audience and addresses her in this speech)*

Hear, Nature, hear, dear goddess, hear!
Suspend thy purpose, if thou didst intend
To make this creature fruitful.

Into her womb convey sterility,
Dry up in her the organs of increase,
And from her derogate body never spring
A babe to honor her! If she must teem,
Create her child of spleen, that it may live
And be a thwart disnatur'd torment to her.
Let it stamp wrinkles in her brow of youth,
With cadent tears fret channels in her cheeks,
Turn all her mother's pains and benefits
To laughter and contempt, that she may feel
How sharper than a serpent's tooth it is
To have a thankless child!—Away, away!

SECOND PLAYER: At the end, when Lear finds that it is Cordelia after all who loved him and that he has been blind about himself as well, his knowledge comes too late. Cordelia and the Fool are dead. Lear comes on stage with the body of his beloved Cordelia in his arms.

(He kneels and leans over an imagined CORDELIA.*)*

LEAR: Howl, howl, howl! O, you are men of stones!
Had I your tongues and eyes, I'd use them so
That heaven's vault should crack. She's gone for ever!
I know when one is dead, and when one lives;
She's dead as earth. Lend me a looking-glass,
If that her breath will mist or stain the stone,
Why then she lives.

. . . .

This feather stirs, she lives! If it be so,
It is a chance which does redeem all sorrows
That ever I have felt.

. . . .

A plague upon you, murderers, traitors all!
I might have sav'd her, now she's gone for ever!
Cordelia, Cordelia, stay a little. Ha!
What is't thou say'st? Her voice was ever soft,
Gentle, and low, an excellent thing in woman.
I kill'd the slave that was a-hanging thee.

. . . .

And my poor fool is hang'd! No, no, no life!
Why should a dog, a horse, a rat, have life,

And thou no breath at all? Thou'lt come no more,
Never, never, never, never, never.
Pray you, undo this button. Thank you, sir.
Do you see this? Look on her! Look her lips,
Look there, look there!

[*He dies*]

SECOND PLAYER: And so the old king dies. Lear's foolish actions helped bring down great evil upon himself and his loved ones, but Lear meant well. Not so Lady Macbeth, whose ambitions for her husband to be king lead her to drive her husband to murder. The three weird sisters have foretold kingship for Macbeth and he has written to tell his wife the news.

(FOURTH PLAYER *becomes* LADY MACBETH, FIRST PLAYER *the* MESSENGER, *and the* THIRD PLAYER MACBETH.)

LADY MACBETH: [*reads*] "They met me in the day of success; and I have learn'd by the perfect'st report, they have more in them than mortal knowledge. When I burnt in desire to question them further, they made themselves air, into which they vanish'd. Whiles I stood rapt in the wonder of it, came missives from the King, who all-hailed me 'Thane of Cawdor,' by which title, before, these weird sisters saluted me, and referr'd me to the coming on of time with 'Hail, King that shalt be!' This have I thought good to deliver thee, my dearest partner of greatness, that thou mightst not lose the dues of rejoicing by being ignorant of what greatness is promis'd thee. Lay it to thy heart, and farewell."
Glamis thou art, and Cawdor, and shalt be
What thou art promis'd. Yet do I fear thy nature,
It is too full o' the milk of human kindness
To catch the nearest way. Thou wouldst be great,
Art not without ambition, but without
The illness should attend it. What thou wouldst highly,
That wouldst thou holily; wouldst not play false,
And yet wouldst wrongly win. Thou'ldst have, great Glamis,
That which cries "Thus thou must do," if thou have it;
And that which rather thou dost fear to do
Than wishest should be undone. Hie thee hither,
That I may pour my spirits in thine ear,
And chastise with the valor of my tongue

All that impedes thee from the golden round,
Which fate and metaphysical aid doth seem
To have thee crown'd withal.

[*Enter* MESSENGER]

What is your tidings?

MESSENGER: The king comes here to-night.

LADY MACBETH: Thou'rt mad to say it!
Is not thy master with him? who, were 't so,
Would have inform'd for preparation.

MESSENGER: So please you, it is true; our thane is coming.
One of my fellows had the speed of him,
Who, almost dead for breath, had scarcely more
Than would make up his message.

LADY MACBETH: Give him tending,
He brings great news.

[*Exit* MESSENGER]

The raven himself is hoarse
That croaks the fatal entrance of Duncan
Under my battlements. Come, you spirits
That tend on mortal thoughts, unsex me here,
And fill me from the crown to the toe topfull
Of direst cruelty! Make thick my blood,
Stop up th' access and passage to remorse,
That no conpunctious visitings of nature
Shake my fell purpose, nor keep peace between
The effect and it! Come to my woman's breasts,
And take my milk for gall, you murth'ring ministers,
Wherever in your sightless substances
You wait on nature's mischief! Come, thick night,
And pall thee in the dunnest smoke of hell,
That my keen knife see not the wound it makes
Nor heaven peep through the blanket of the dark,
To cry, "Hold, hold!"

SECOND PLAYER: Evil returns upon itself, though, and all turns to ashes for Lady Macbeth and her husband. Finally when he hears of his wife's death, Macbeth sees nothing before him but emptiness and despair.

MACBETH: She should have died hereafter;
There would have been a time for such a word.

To-morrow, and to-morrow, and to-morrow,
Creeps in this petty pace from day to day,
To the last syllable of recorded time;
And all our yesterdays have lighted fools
The way to dusty death. Out, out, brief candle!
Life's but a walking shadow, a poor player
That struts and frets his hour upon the stage,
And then is heard no more. It is a tale
Told by an idiot, full of sound and fury,
Signifying nothing.

FOURTH PLAYER: True to the life his art reflects, Shakespeare often mixes tragedy and comedy in his plays. Hamlet, the young prince who gave advice to the players, pretends to be mad so that he can find out his father's murderer, Claudius, more easily. Polonius, an aging, somewhat senile courtier, and Claudius' spy, suspects the madness comes from despair over Polonius's own daughter, Ophelia, whom Hamlet loves.

(FIRST PLAYER *becomes* POLONIUS, *the* SECOND PLAYER, *taking a book from the box-bench, becomes* HAMLET.)

POLONIUS: How does my good Lord Hamlet.

(HAMLET *reclines on the box-bench, reading.*)

HAMLET: Well, God-a-mercy.
POLONIUS: Do you know me, my lord?
HAMLET: Excellent well, you are a fishmonger.
POLONIUS: Not I, my lord.
HAMLET: Then I would you were so honest a man.
POLONIUS: Honest, my lord?

(HAMLET *rises and stands over* POLONIUS *on the box-bench.*)

HAMLET: Ay, sir, to be honest, as this world goes, is to be one man pick'd out of ten thousand.
POLONIUS: That's very true, my lord.
HAMLET: For if the sun breed maggots in a dead dog, being a good kissing carrion—Have you a daughter?
POLONIUS: I have, my lord.
HAMLET: Let her not walk i' the sun. Conception is a blessing, but as your daughter may conceive, friend, look to 't.
POLONIUS: [*Aside*] How say you by that? still harping on my daughter. Yet he knew me not at first, 'a said I was a

fishmonger. 'A is far gone. And truly in my youth I suff'red much extremity for love—very near this. I'll speak to him again.—What do you read, my lord?

(HAMLET *descends*)

HAMLET: Words, words, words.

POLONIUS: What is the matter, my lord?

HAMLET: Between who?

POLONIUS: I mean, the matter that you read, my lord.

HAMLET: Slanders, sir; for the satirical rogue says here that old men have grey beards, that their faces are wrinkled, their eyes purging thick amber and plumtree gum, and that they have a plentiful lack of wit, together with most weak hams; all which, sir, though I most powerfully and potently believe, yet I hold it not honesty to have it thus set down, for yourself, sir, shall grow old as I am, if like a crab you could go backward.

POLONIUS: [*Aside*] Though this be madness, yet there is method in 't.—Will you walk out of the air, my lord?

HAMLET: Into my grave.

POLONIUS: Indeed, that's out of the air. [*Aside*] How pregnant sometimes his replies are! a happiness that often madness hits on, which reason and sanity could not so prosperously be deliver'd of. I will leave him, and suddenly contrive the means of meeting between him and my daughter.—My lord, I will take my leave of you.

HAMLET: You cannot, take from me any thing that I will more willingly part withal—except my life, except my life, except my life.

POLONIUS: Fare you well, my lord.

HAMLET: These tedious old fools!

(SECOND PLAYER *sings "What A Piece of Work Is Man" from the rock musical, HAIR.*)

FOURTH PLAYER: But now, like King Theseus at the end of *A Midsummer Night's Dream,* we must bid one another good night—knowing perhaps, that all life reflected in Shakespeare's mirror may be but a dream. And you and I, in Prospero's words, may be

such stuff

As dreams are made on; and our little life
Is rounded with a sleep.

(FIRST PLAYER *becomes* THESEUS, SECOND PLAYER PUCK, THIRD PLAYER OBERON, *the* FOURTH PLAYER, TITANIA.)

THESEUS: The iron tongue of midnight hath told twelve.
Lovers, to bed, 'tis almost fairy time.
I fear we shall outsleep the coming morn
As much as we this night have overwatch'd.
This palpable-gross play hath well beguil'd
The heavy gait of night. Sweet friends, to bed.
A fortnight hold we this solemnity,
In nightly revels and new jollity.
PUCK: Now the hungry lion roars,
And the wolf behowls the moon;
Whilst the heavy ploughman snores,
All with weary task fordone.
Now the wasted brands do glow,
Whilst the screech-owl, screeching loud,
Puts the wretch that lies in woe
In remembrance of a shroud.
Now it is the time of night
That the graves, all gaping wide,
Every one lets forth his sprite,
In the church-way paths to glide
And we fairies, that do run
By the triple Hecate's team
From the presence of the sun,
Following darkness like a dream,
Now are frolic. Not a mouse
Shall disturb this hallowed house.
I am sent with broom before,
To sweep the dust behind the door.
OBERON: Through the house give glimmering light
By the dead and drowsy fire.
Every elf and fairy sprite
Hop as light as bird from brier,
And this ditty, after me,
Sing, and dance it trippingly.

TITANIA: First, rehearse your song by rote,
To each word a warbling note.
Hand in hand, with fairy grace,
Will we sing, and bless this place.

(The FOUR PLAYERS *sing "Where The Bee Sucks" from THE TEMPEST.)*

FOUR PLAYERS: Where the bee sucks, there suck I,
In a cowslip's bell I lie;
There I couch when owls do cry.
On the bat's back I do fly
After summer merrily,
Merrily, merrily shall I live now,
Under the blossom that hangs on the bough.

OBERON: Now, until the break of day,
Through this house each fairy stray.
To the best bride-bed will we,
Which by us shall blessed be;
And the issue, there create,
Ever shall be fortunate.
So shall all the couples three
Ever true in loving be;
And the blots of Nature's hand
Shall not in their issue stand;
Never mole, hare lip, nor scar,
Nor mark prodigious, such as are
Despised in nativity,
Shall upon their children be.
With this field-dew consecrate,
Every fairy take his gait,
And each several chamber bless,
Through this palace, with sweet peace,
And the owner of it blest,
Ever shall in safety rest.
Trip away; make no stay;
Meet me all by break of day.

PUCK: If we shadows have offended,
Think but this, and all is mended,
That you have but slumb'red here,
While these visions did appear.

And this weak and idle theme,
No more yielding but a dream,
Gentles, do not reprehend.
If you pardon, we will mend.
And, as I am an honest Puck,
If we have unearned luck
Now to scape the serpent's tongue,
We will make amends ere long;
Else the Puck a liar call.
So, good night unto you all.
Give me your hands, if we be friends,
And Robin shall restore amends.

(*The* FOUR PLAYERS *exit singing the opening song—but now with its proper ending.*)

FOUR PLAYERS: But that's all one, our play is done,
And we'll strive to please you every day.

A CANTERBURY CAPER

(A dramatic adaptation of Chauncer's *The Canterbury Tales)*

In making my adaptation, I have used Theodore Morrison's translation of *The Canterbury Tales* into modern English in *The Portable Chaucer,* selected, translated, and edited by Theodore Morrison, The Viking Press, New York City, 1949. The adaptation, however, is a rather free one with the material sometimes presented in a nonlinear fashion, a speech occasionally given to a different character than one who originally spoke it or sometimes divided up among several characters, in each case for dramatic reasons. Other changes in wording also are necessary to the dramatic form. The stage directions are, of course, my own.

K.H.B.

Dramatis Personae

First Player: Alison in "The Miller's Tale," Jew and Christian in "The Prioress' Tale," Wife of Bath and Old Woman in "The Wife of Bath's Tale," Servant and Apothecary in "The Pardoner's Tale," Dame Partlet in "The Nun's Priest's Tale."

Second Player: Chaucer, Miller, Carpenter in "The Miller's Tale," Jew and Christian in "The Prioress' Tale," A Husband, Guard, and Woods in "The Wife of Bath's Tale," Rioter One in "The Pardoner's Tale," Chanticleer in "The Nun's Priest's Tale."

Third Player: Host, Nicholas in "The Miller's Tale," Child in "The Prioress' Tale," A Husband and the Knight in "The Wife of Bath's Tale," Rioter Two in "The Pardoner's Tale," The Priest who tells "The Nun's Priest's Tale."

Fourth Player: Jervice in "The Miller's Tale," Raped Maiden, Queen, and Ladies in "The Wife of Bath's Tale," Prioress and Widow in "The Prioress' Tale," Rioter Three in "The Pardoner's Tale," Widow in "The Nun's Priest's Tale."

Fifth Player: Absolom in "The Miller's Tale," Jew and Christian in "The Prioress' Tale," Fifth Husband, Guard, and Woods in "The Wife of Bath's Tale," Pardoner and Old Man in "The Pardoner's Tale," Fox in "The Nun's Priest's Tale."

Scenery: The stage is set with three ladders, one of which is slightly taller than the others. The ladders are continually rearranged to meet setting needs, and pillows of different sizes and shapes are used as all properties. The ladders, pillows, and costumes are red, purple, yellow, and green—all suggestive of spring.

As the lights come up flute music is heard and the FIRST PLAYER *emerges from backstage to climb center stage ladder. She recites the opening of the Prologue in Middle English with great seriousness. The other* PLAYERS *come running on from the audience, yelping, carrying each other, and generally carrying on. Perplexed, the* FIRST PLAYER *continues while the others increase their wild behavior and noises. As she finishes the eighteenth line, the* FIRST PLAYER *gives up, decides to join in, and jumps into the arms of the others, who fall with her weight to the ground. The* SECOND PLAYER *emerges as* CHAUCER, *climbs the center stage ladder, and begins the Prologue in modern English. The other* PLAYERS *lie at his feet, kicking their own feet in the air, but as he continues they rise slowly, as if being born as part of spring.*

CHAUCER: As soon as April pierces to the root
The drought of March, and bathes each bud and shoot
Through every vein of sap with gentle showers
From whose engendering liquor spring the flowers;
When zephyrs have breathed softly all about
Inspiring every wood and field to sprout,
And in the zodiac the youthful sun
His journey halfway through the Ram has run;
When little birds are busy with their song
Who sleep with open eyes the whole night long
Life stirs their hearts and tingles in them so,
Then off as pilgrims people long to go,
And palmers to set out for distant strands
And foreign shrines renowned in many lands.

(*The* PLAYERS *turn into* PILGRIMS *riding their horses and do an abstract meeting and greeting dance here.*)

And specially in England people ride
To Canterbury from every countryside
To visit there the blessed martyred saint
Who gave them strength when they were sick and faint.

(FIFTH PLAYER *plays riding music on recorder.*)

In Southwark at the Tabard one spring day
It happened, as I stopped there on my way,
Myself a pilgrim with a heart devout
Ready for Canterbury to set out,
At night came all of twenty-nine assorted
Travelers, and to that same inn resorted,
Who by a turn of fortune chanced to fall
In fellowship together, and they were all
Pilgrims who had it in their minds to ride
Toward Canterbury. The stable doors were wide,
The rooms were large, and we enjoyed the best,
And shortly, when the sun had gone to rest,
I had so talked with each that presently
I was a member of their company
And promised to rise early the next day
To start, as I shall show, upon our way.
Our Host gave each of us a cheerful greeting
And promptly of our supper had us eating.
Lacking no trace of manhood, bold in speech,
Prudent, and well versed in what life can teach,
With all of this he was a jovial man.
And so when supper ended he began:

HOST: You go to Canterbury—may the Lord
Speed you, and may the martyred saint reward
Your journey! And to while the time away
You mean to talk and pass the time of day,
For you would be as cheerful all alone
As riding on your journey dumb as stone.
Therefore, if you'll abide by what I say,
Tomorrow, when you ride off on your way,
Now, by my father's soul, and he is dead,
If you don't enjoy yourselves, cut off my head!
Each one of you, to make our journey short,
Shall tell two stories, as we ride, I mean,
Toward Canterbury; and coming home again
Shall tell two other tales he may have heard
Of happenings that some time have occurred.
And the one of you whose stories please us most,

Here in this tavern, sitting by this post
Shall sup at our expense while we make merry
When we come riding home from Canterbury.
And to cheer you still the more, I too will ride
With you at my own cost, and be your guide.
And if anyone my judgment shall gainsay
He must pay for all we spend along the way.
If you agree, no need to stand and reason.
Tell me, and I'll be stirring in good season.

FIFTH PLAYER: This thing is granted, and we swear our pledge
To take your judgment on our pilgrimage.

FOURTH PLAYER: And set the supper at a certain price.

FIRST PLAYER: We promise to be ruled by your advice!

CHAUCER: Next morning, when the dawn was in the east,
Up sprang our Host, who acted as our cock,
And gathered us together in a flock,
And off we rode, till presently our pace
Had brought us to St. Thomas' watering place.

(*The* FIVE PLAYERS *move as if on horseback.*)

The Miller, who by this time was so drunk
He looked quite bloodless, and who hardly sat
His horse, he was never one to doff his hat
Or stand on courtesy for any man.
Like Pilate in the Church plays he began
To bellow!

(CHAUCER *turns into* MILLER *here.*)

MILLER: Everyone listen! But first I will propound
That I am drunk, I know it by my sound.
If I can't get my words out, put the blame
On Southwark ale, I ask you, in God's name!
For I'll tell a golden legend and a life
Both of a carpenter and of his wife,
A student who put horns upon his head . . .

HOST: Shut up, be still, take back what you have said.
Forget your ignorant drunken bawdiness.
It is a sin and a great foolishness
To injure any man by defamation
And to give women such a reputation.
Tell us of other things; you'll find no lack.

MILLER: My brother Host, as true as babes are suckled,
The man who has no wife, he is no cuckold.
There used to be a rich old oaf who made
His home at Oxford, a carpenter by trade,
And took in boarders. With him used to dwell
A student who had done his studies well,
But he was poor; for all that he had learned,
It was toward astrology his fancy turned.

(Indicates himself as CARPENTER *by sawing on ladder with a pillow and introduces* THIRD PLAYER *as* STUDENT. *The* STUDENT *does magic tricks and flirts with the two ladies.)*

He knew a number of figures and constructions
By which he could supply men with deductions
If they should ask him at a given hour
Whether to look for sunshine or for shower,
Or want to know whatever might befall,
Events of all sorts, I can't count them all.
He was known as handy Nicholas, this student.
Well versed in love, he knew how to be prudent,
Going about unnoticed, sly, and sure.
In looks no girl was ever more demure.

(MILLER *pushes* STUDENT *to center ladder, which* STUDENT *climbs: he sits on top.)*

Lodged at this carpenter's, he lived alone;
He had a room there that he made his own,
Festooned with herbs, and he was sweet himself
As licorice or ginger.
This carpenter had newly wed a wife
And loved her better than he loved his life.
He was jealous, for she was eighteen in age;
He tried to keep her close as in a cage,

(MILLER *puts* FIRST PLAYER *as* WIFE *under ladder.)*

For she was wild and young, and old was he
And guessed that he might smack of cuckoldry.
Now listen, gentlemen, to how it was:
A day came round when handy Nicholas,
Her husband being gone at Oseney,
Began to fool with this young wife, and play.

(STUDENT *and* WIFE *flirt by running around and up ladder on either side.*)

NICHOLAS: Sweetheart, unless I have my will with you
I'll die for stifled love, by all that's true,
I vow
I'll die unless you love me here and now!

(*Grabs her at top of ladder.*)

ALISON: I will not kiss you, on my life.
Why, stop it now, oh stop it Nicholas,
Or I will cry out 'Help, help,' and 'Alas!'
Be good enough to take your hands away.

(*A long kiss after which they move slowly down either side of the ladder.*)

I swear to you, I give my solemn promise
To be at your disposal by St. Thomas,
When I can spy an opportunity.
My husband is so full of jealousy,
Unless you watch your step and hold your breath
I know for certain it will be my death.

(*They try to kiss through rungs of ladder, give up, and shake hands.*)

NICHOLAS: A student has been wasting time at school
If he can't make a carpenter a fool.

MILLER: Now in her Christian duty, one saint's day,
To the parish church this good wife made her way,
And as she went her forehead cast a glow
As bright as noon, for she had washed it so
It glistened when she finished with her work.

(WIFE *and* FOURTH PLAYER *sit on step of ladder and do prayers.* FIFTH PLAYER *becomes* ABSOLOM. *He has been sitting stage right and now as the* MILLER *crosses to him and describes him, he kneels, preens, and dances all around. He carries a guitar.*)

Serving this church there was a parish clerk
Whose name was Absolom, a ruddy man
With goose-gray eyes and curls like a great fan
That shone like gold on his neatly parted head.
His tunic was light blue and his nose red,
And he had patterns that had been cut through

Like the windows of St. Paul's in either shoe.
A merry devil, as true as God can save,
He knew how to let blood, trim hair, and shave,
Or write a deed of land in proper phrase,
And he could dance in twenty different ways
In the Oxford fashion, and sometimes he would sing
A loud falsetto to his fiddle string
Or his guitar. No tavern anywhere
But he had furnished entertainment there.
Censing the parish women one and all,
Many the doting look that he let fall,
But with a heartful of love-hankerings
He would not take the women's offerings;
No, no, he said, it would not be polite.

(*Taking the collection with his guitar,* ABSOLOM *approaches the* FOURTH PLAYER *but he will take nothing from her. Then he sees* ALISON *and plunks guitar as he falls in love. The* PLAYERS *set other two ladders next to tall one to be house.* ALISON *and* MILLER *as* CARPENTER *climb short ladders, sit on their tops and cover selves with quilt—look as if in bed.*)

The moon, when darkness fell, shone full and bright,
And Absolom was ready for love's sake
With his guitar to be up and awake,
And toward the carpenter's, brisk and amorous,
He made his way until he reached the house
A little after the cocks began to crow.
Under a casement he sang sweet and low:

ABSOLOM: Now, lady dear, I pray that you will be
Tender and kind to one who loves—that's me.

CARPENTER: (*Waking up.*) Alison!
Wife! Do you hear him? There goes Absolom—
Absolom singing under our bedroom wall?

ALISON: Yes, God knows, John, I hear it all.

(*They go back to sleep. Cock crows, they waken, descend, and* CARPENTER *goes up large ladder to look for* NICHOLAS.)

CARPENTER: What, how, what's doing, Master Nicholas?
How can you sleep all day? Get up, you must!
(*to wife.*) The man's astronomy has turned his wit,

Or else he's in some agonizing fit.
What, how! What is it? Look down at us!
Wake up, think of Christ's passion, Nicholas!

(They press in an imaginary door with pillow.)

NICHOLAS: Alas,
This world, must it be all destroyed straightway?
CARPENTER: What, what's that you say?
Do as we do, we working men, and think
Of God. Don't sit around and sigh.
NICHOLAS: Now, John, you must believe this is no lie.
I have discovered through astrology
And studying the moon that shines so bright
That Monday next, a quarter through the night,
A rain will fall, and such a mad, wild spate
That Noah's flood was never half so great.
This world, my friends, in less time than an hour
Shall drown entirely in that hideous shower.
Yes, every man shall drown and lose his life.
CARPENTER: Alas, then for my wife!
Alas, my Alison! And shall she drown?
But is there nothing to be done?
NICHOLAS: If you will act on good advice, no fail,
I'll promise, and without a mast or sail,
To see that she's preserved, and you and I.
Haven't you heard how Noah was kept dry
When warned by Christ beforehand, he discovered
That the whole earth with water should be covered?
Start out and get into the house right off
For each of us a tub or kneading-trough,
Above all making sure that they are large,
In which we'll float away as in a barge.

(CARPENTER *brings three pillows which they arrange as boat, using a fourth as an oar—all climb in and* CARPENTER *rows.*)

And put in food enough to last a day.
Beyond won't matter, the flood will fall away
Early next morning. Take care not to spill
A word to your boy Robin, nor to Jill
Your maid. I cannot save her, don't ask why.
I will not tell God's secrets, no, not I.
Let it be enough, unless your wits are mad,

To have as good a grace as Noah had.
I'll save your wife for certain, never doubt it.

(*Kisses her when* CARPENTER *is busy rowing.*)

Now go along, and make good time about it.
But when you have, for her and you and me,
Brought to the house these kneading-tubs, all three,
Then you must hang them under the roof, up high,
To keep our plans from any watchful eye.
Go now, the plans are drawn.
Go, set to work, and may God spur you on!

ALISON: (*Pretends to be dead with fright.*)
Alas, go get this business done.
Help us escape, or we are dead, each one.
I am true, your faithful wedded wife.
Go, my dear husband, save us, limb and life!

(ALISON *kisses* NICHOLAS *while* CARPENTER *brings pillows which they then distribute and all go to sleep;* NICHOLAS *sleeps on top of tall ladder,* ALISON *and the* CARPENTER *on top of two other ladders representing their bed. They kiss and disappear behind the quilt which they hold up in front of themselves. The* CARPENTER *snores loudly after which* ALISON *joins* NICHOLAS.)

ABSOLOM: What has become of John the Carpenter?
That he's away is all I can infer,
For certainly I haven't seen him making
A stir about his door since day was breaking.
Don't call me a man if when I hear the cock
Begin to crow I don't slip up and knock
On the low window by his bedroom wall.
To Alison at last I'll pour out all
My love-pangs, for at this point I can't miss,
Whatever happens, at the least a kiss.
Some comfort, by my word, will come my way.
I've felt my mouth itch the whole livelong day,
And that's a sign of kissing at the least.
I dreamed all night that I was at a feast.

(*Moves to ladders center.*)

My honeycomb, sweet Alison,
What are you doing, my sweet cinnamon?
Awake, my sweetheart and my pretty bird,

Awake, and give me from your lips a word!
Little enough you care for all my woe,
How for your love I sweat wherever I go!

ALISON: You jack-fool, get away from here!
So help me God, I won't sing "Kiss me, dear!"
I love another more than you. Get on,
For Christ's sake, Absolom, or I'll throw a stone.
The devil with you! Go and let me sleep.

ABSOLOM: Ah, that true love should ever have to reap
So evil a fortune. Give me a kiss,
At least, if it can be no more than this,
Give it, for love of Jesus and of me.

ALISON: And if I do, will you be off at once?

ABSOLOM: Promise you, darling, promise you Alison.

ALISON: (*to* NICHOLAS.) Keep still,
And in a minute you can laugh your fill.

(*Using tall ladder, pretends to open window under it and puts her rear end out.*)

Be quick about it, and be spry
For fear the neighbors will look out and spy.

(ABSOLOM *wipes mouth dry, kisses rear.*)

ABSOLOM: Something is amiss.
This could not be my Alison I kiss.
A woman has no beard, I'm well aware,
But what I felt was rough and had long hair.

ALISON: (*Claps window down, runs back up to* NICHOLAS.)
Teehee!

ABSOLOM: Alas, alas! What is it I have done?

NICHOLAS: A beard, a beard! God's body this is fun.

ABSOLOM: The devil
Welcome my soul if I wouldn't rather be
Revenged than have the whole town in a sack!
Alas, if only I'd held back!

(FOURTH PLAYER *becomes* JERVICE *at whose door* ABSOLOM *knocks stage left.*)

Undo the door, Jervice, and let me come.

JERVICE: What? Who are you?

ABSOLOM: It is I, Absolom.

JERVICE: Absolom, is it! By Christ's precious tree,

Why are you up so early? Lord bless me,
What's ailing you? Some gay girl has the power
To bring you out, God knows, at such an hour!
Yes, by St. Neot, you know well what I mean!

ABSOLOM: (*Takes long red pillow.*) Lend me this colter here
That's hot in the chimney, friend, don't fear,
I'll bring it back right off when I am through.
I need it for a job I have to do.

JERVICE: Of course, my friend, why, if it were all gold
Or coins in a sack, uncounted and untold,
As I'm a rightful smith, I wouldn't refuse it.
But, Christ's foot! how on earth do you mean to use it?

ABSOLOM: Let that be as it may.
I'll let you know tomorrow or next day.

(*Creeps to* ALISON'S *window, coughs again, knocks, gives little call just as did before.*)

ALISON: Who's knocking there?
It is a thief, I swear.

ABSOLOM: No, no, God knows, my sugarplum,
My bird, my darling, it's your Absolom.
I've brought a golden ring my mother gave me,
Fine and well cut, as I hope that God will save me.
It's yours, if you will let me have a kiss.
Speak, for I don't know where you are, sweetheart.

(NICHOLAS *descends, opens window, puts rear out,* ABSOLOM *strikes with pillow.*)

NICHOLAS: Help! Water! Water! Help, for God's own heart!

CARPENTER: (*Waking.*) Alas, it's Noah's flood, we'd better start.

(*General chaos and running about ladders:* CARPENTER *falls to ground and rows while others carry on. During chaos they change ladders so that one is up stage right, one is up stage left, and one is down stage left.*)

CHAUCER: Served in this fashion was the carpenter's wife,
And everyone was laughing at the strife.
In spite of all his jealousy could try.

ABSOLOM: And Absolom has kissed her nether eye.

NICHOLAS: And Nicholas was scaulded on the bum.

ALL: That's all the tale, God save us, every one!

(The PLAYERS *take positions of prayer on their knees with above lines. The following tale should be acted in terms of the image of children's games, partly because the tale is about a child, but partly because of the childlike nature of the* PRIORESS *and her tale with its simplified view of good and evil. The* FOURTH PLAYER *becomes* PRIORESS.)

PRIORESS: *(kneeling stage left.)*
O Lord, our Lord, how marvelously thy name
Is spread abroad for this wide world, to see.
Not only are thy praise and precious fame
Wrought on the earth by men of dignity,
But children's mouths proclaim thine excellency,
For often the mere suckling at the breast
Thy bounty and thy praise will manifest.
Wherefore in praise, after my best endeavor,
Of thee and the white lily that in her hour
Brought thee to birth, and is a maid forever,
A story shall I tell, though with no power
To increase her honor, she the unsoiled flower
Who in herself is honor; they are one;
Soul's blessing, and root of mercy, next her Son.

(During the following description, the PRIORESS *does a dance amidst the kneeling* PILGRIMS.)

CHAUCER: There was also a Nun, a Prioress,
Whose smile was gentle and full of guilelessness.
"By St. Loy!" was the worst oath she would say.
She sang mass well, in a becoming way,
Intoning through her nose the words divine,
THIRD PLAYER: And she was known as Madame Eglantine.
She spoke good French, as taught at Stratford-Bow,
PRIORESS: For the Parisian French I do not know.
FIRST PLAYER: She was schooled to eat so primly and so well
That from her lips no morsel ever fell.
She wet her fingers lightly in the dish
Of sauce, for courtesy was her first wish.
With every bite she did her skillful best
To see that no drop fell upon her breast.
FIFTH PLAYER: She was a great delight, and always tried
To imitate court ways, and had her pride,
Both amiable and gracious in her dealings.

CHAUCER: As for her charity and tender feelings,
She melted at whatever was piteous.
She would weep if she but came upon a mouse
Caught in a trap, if it were dead or bleeding.
THIRD PLAYER: Some little dogs that she took pleasure feeding
On roasted meat or milk or good wheat bread
She had, but how she wept to find one dead
FIFTH PLAYER: Or yelping from a blow that made it smart,
ALL: And all was sympathy and loving heart.
PRIORESS: So weak, O happy Queen, is all my art
To show forth thine exceeding worthiness
I cannot bear the weight upon my heart,
But as a child of twelve months' age or less
Who scarcely can a single word express,
Just so I fare, and so to thee I pray
Direct this song of you that I shall say.

(PRIORESS *stage right, takes* THIRD PLAYER *with her to ladder; he sits at her feet, she on a rung of the ladder.*)

In a great city of Asia, right among
Good Christian people, once there used to be
A ghetto, kept by a local lord who wrung
Foul profit from it, and wretched usury,
Hateful to Christ and to his company.
And through the street men freely rode or went;
At either end was nothing to prevent.

(*Indicates* FIRST PLAYER, CHAUCER, *and* HOST, *who become the* JEWS. *They play children's games in slow motion dance.* PRIORESS *becomes* WIDOW, THIRD PLAYER *her* SON.)

WIDOW: Now as you go to school my little one,
I want you to behave as you've been told.
If you should happen to behold
An image of Christ's Mother, then kneel and say
Hail Mary as you go upon your way.

(*She sings "O Alma Redemptoris."*)

BOY: What does this song mean, and why is it in use?
WIDOW: This song, as I have heard them say,
Was made about our blessed Lady, she
Who is gracious ever, to honor her, and pray
That she will be our help in our last day.

BOY: And was this song made up in reverence
Of Christ's dear mother?
Now certainly, with all my diligence,
I'll learn it before Christmastide is gone.
Punish me when my primer isn't done
Or beat me thrice an hour though they do,
To honor our Lady I'll learn it all right through.

(The BOY *goes off to school singing "O Alma.")*

FIRST PLAYER *as* JEW: O Hebrew people, is it for the best
That a mere boy, just as he likes, should tread
Your street, and bring contempt upon your head,
And sing to such a purpose, for a cause
That is against the reverence of your laws?

(The JEWS *involve* BOY *in their games, then kill him. He sings the entire time, stops briefly as he dies, then sings again.)*

WIDOW: And have you seen my child go by, kind Sir?

(Repeats line three times as seeks CHILD. *The* THREE JEWS *turn into sympathetic* CHRISTIANS *and help her search. They find the dead* BOY *singing.)*

O great God, whose perfection is extolled
By praise of innocents, here shows thy might!
This gem of chastity, this emerald
And ruby of martyrdom, unstained and bright,
Lying with carven throat and out of sight,
Is singing out *O Alma* from the ground
And all the place is ringing with the sound.

(They place BOY *on ladder which has been put on its side like a bier, all singing "O Alma.")*

SECOND PLAYER *as kind* CHRISTIAN: Dear child, enlighten me,
By virtue of the Holy Trinity,
How can you sing thus, when to my poor eye
Your throat is cut, unless my senses lie.

BOY: My throat is cut clear down to the neck-bone,
Such is the nature of mankind
I should have died long since by that alone.
But it is written in books, as you may find,
That Christ will have his glory kept in mind,
And for the worship of his mother dear

I still may sing *O Alma* loud and clear.
As well as I knew how, the sweet renown
Of Christ's dear mother, mercy's well and spring,
I loved, and when the time came to lay down
My life, she came to me and bade me sing
This anthem in my hour of perishing;
And then it seemed that after I had sung
She laid a grain of pearl upon my tongue.
And so I sing, and sing I must, indeed,
In honor always of that blessed Maid,
Until some hand has taken away the seed
Of pearl that here upon my tongue she laid.
"My little child," she said, "be not afraid,
For I will come for you when they have taken
This grain away; you shall not be forsaken."

(SECOND PLAYER *removes seed from tongue and* BOY *stops singing. The* PLAYERS *carry him up stage on ladder and all collect pillows, remove down stage right ladder to upstage right, then stand with backs to audience in preparation for* WIFE OF BATH *as* PRIORESS *addresses audience about Hugh of Lincoln.*)

PRIORESS: Young Hugh of Lincoln, you were also
Slain by accursed Jews, notoriously,
For it was but a little while ago,
Pray for us; in our fitful errancy,
We sinful folk, that God will mercifully,
In honor of her that Christ our Saviour bore,
Multiply mercy to us evermore!
Amen.

(*As* PRIORESS *repeats another "Amen," the* FIRST PLAYER *kneels down stage right, other* PLAYERS *all yelp, rush forth and cover her with pillows from which she emerges, rear first, as the* WIFE OF BATH.)

WIFE OF BATH: Lords, since I was twelve years old
—Thanks to eternal God in heaven alive—
I have married at church door no less than five
Husbands, provided that I can have been
So often wed, and all were worthy men.
But plainly, this I know without a lie,
God told us to increase and multiply.

Blessed be God that I have married five,
Welcome the sixth, as long as I'm alive.

(WIFE OF BATH *freezes.* FIFTH HUSBAND *sits on ladder down stage left and reads from a pillow which represents a book as she tells of others.*)

FIFTH HUSBAND: "Build a foundation over sands or shallows,
Or gallop a blind horse across the fallows,
Let a wife traipse to shrines that some saint hallows,
And you are fit to swing upon the gallows."

WIFE OF BATH: In wifehood I will use my instrument
As freely by my Maker it was lent.
If I hold back with it, God give me sorrow!
My husband shall enjoy it night and morrow
When it pleases him to come and pay his debt.
But a husband, and I've not been thwarted yet,
Shall always be my debtor and my slave.
From tribulation he shall never save
His flesh, not for as long as I'm his wife!
I have the power, during all my life,
Over his very body, and not he.
For so the Apostle has instructed me,
Who bade men love their wives for better or worse.
It pleases me from end to end, that verse!

(*She freezes.*)

FIFTH HUSBAND: Now first I'll read of Eve, whose wickedness
Delivered all mankind to wretchedness
For which in his own person Christ was slain
Who with his heart's blood bought us all again.
By this, I say, expressly you may find
That woman was the loss of all mankind.

THIRD PLAYER: Go on as you began!
Tell us your tale, spare not for any man.
Instruct us younger men who need a guide.

WIFE OF BATH: Gladly, if it will please you, to abide,
But first I ask you, if I speak my mind,
That all this company may be well inclined,
And will not take offense at what I say.
I only mean it, after all, in play.
Now, sirs, I will get onward with my tale.

If ever I hope to drink good wine or ale,
I'm speaking truth: the husbands I have had,
Three of them have been good, and two were bad.
The three were kindly men, and rich, and old.
But they were hardly able to uphold
The statute which had made them fast to me.
You know well what I mean by this, I see!
So help me God, I can't help laughing yet
When I think of how at night I made them sweat,
And since I had them wholly in my hand
And they had given me their wealth and land,
Why task myself to spoil them or to please
Unless for my own profit and my ease?
They were glad to bring me trinkets from the fair
And happy when I spoke with a mild air,
For God knows I could chide outrageously,
Now judge if I could do it properly!

(SECOND *and* THIRD PLAYERS *become the* HUSBANDS.)

(*To* SECOND PLAYER.) "Sir dotard, this is how you live?" I'd say.
"How can my neighbor's wife be dressed so gay?
She carries off the honors everywhere.
I sit at home. I've nothing fit to wear.
What were you doing at my neighbor's house?
Is she so handsome? Are you so amorous?
What do you whisper to our maid? God bless me,
Give up your jokes, old lecher. They depress me.
(*To* THIRD PLAYER.) That chest of yours, why do you hide the keys
Away from me? It's my wealth, if you please,
As much as yours. Will you make a fool of me,
The mistress of our house? You shall not be
Lord of my body and my wealth at once!"
And thus in one point I can take just pride:
In the end I showed myself the stronger side.

(*She freezes.*)

FIFTH HUSBAND: Have you read too how Samson as he slept
Was shorn of all his hair by her he kept,

And by that treachery Samson lost his eyes.
Delilah was the cause, I'll tell no lies.

WIFE OF BATH: This was the way I talked when I had need.
But now to my fourth husband I'll proceed.
This fourth I married was a roisterer.
He had a mistress, and my passions were,
Although I say it, strong; and altogether
I was young and stubborn, pert in every feather.
I paid him for this debt; I made it good.
I furnished him a cross of the same wood,
By God and by St. Joce—in no foul fashion,
Not with my flesh; but I put on such passion
And rendered him so jealous, I'll engage
I made him fry in his own grease for rage!
On earth, God Knows, I was his purgatory;
I only hope his soul is now in glory.
He died when I came home from Jerusalem.
He's buried near the chancel, under a beam.
And so to church my husband on the morrow
Was borne away by neighbors in their sorrow.
Jenkin, the student, was among the crowd,
And when I saw him walk, so help me God,
Behind the bier, I thought he had a pair
Of legs and feet so cleanly turned and fair
I put my heart completely in his hold.
He was in fact some twenty winters old
And I was forty, to confess the truth;
But all my life I've had a wild colt's tooth.
My teeth were spaced apart; that was the seal
St. Venus printed, and became me well.
So help me God, I was a lusty one,
Pretty and young and rich, and full of fun.
For I belong to Venus in my feelings,
Though I bring the heart of Mars to all my dealings.
From Venus come my lust and appetite,
From Mars I get my courage and my might,
Born under Taurus, while Mars stood therein.
Alas, alas, that ever love was sin!
What should I say, but when the month ran out,

This jolly student, always much about,
This Jenkin married me in solemn state.
To him I gave land, titles, the whole slate
Of goods that had been given me before;
But my repentance afterward was sore!

SECOND, THIRD, *and* FOURTH PLAYERS: By God madam, this is a long preamble to a tale.

WIFE OF BATH: And now of my fifth husband let me tell.
God never let his soul go down to hell
Though he of all five was my scourge and flail!
I feel it on my ribs, right down the scale,
And ever shall until my dying day.
And yet he was so full of life and gay
In bed, and could so melt me and cajole me
When on my back he had a mind to roll me,
What matter if on every bone he'd beaten me!
He'd have my love, so quickly he could sweeten me.
He had a book, *Valerious,* he called it,
And Theophrastus, and he always hauled it
From where it lay to read both day and night
And laughed hard at it, such was his delight.
He dredged this book for tales of wicked wives.
He knew more stories of their wretched lives
Than are told about good women in the Bible.

ALL: By God, madam . . .this is a long preamble to a tale!

WIFE OF BATH: But now for the story that I undertook—
To tell how I was beaten for a book.
Jenkin, one night, who never seemed to tire
Of reading in his book, sat by the fire

(She freezes.)

FIFTH HUSBAND: I'll tell you now of Clytemnestra's lechery
And how she killed her husband off by treachery.
And wives in recent times it's said
Have sometimes murdered husbands when in bed.
And all night long have let a paramour
Enjoy them with the corpse flat on the floor;
Better a dragon for a mate,
Better on a lion's whims to wait
Than on a wife whose way it is to chide.

Better high in the loft to bide
Than with a railing wife down in the house.
They are so wicked and cantankerous.

(FIFTH HUSBAND'S *last speech and* WIFE'S *following one overlap: his should be muted as he reads from ladder.*)

WIFE OF BATH: Who could imagine, who would half suppose
The gall my heart drank, raging at each drop?
And when I saw that he would never stop
Reading all night from his accursed book,
Suddenly, in the midst of it, I took
Three leaves and tore them out in a great pique,
And with my fist I caught him on the cheek
So hard he tumbled backward in the fire.
And up he jumped, he was as mad for ire
As a mad lion, and caught me on the head
With such a blow I fell down as if dead.
And seeing me on the floor, how still I lay,
He was aghast, and would have fled away,
Till I came to at length, and gave a cry.

(WIFE OF BATH *plays both roles until she comes to; then* FIFTH HUSBAND *descends ladder and cradles her in his arms.*)

Have you killed me for my lands? Before I die,
False thief, I'll give you a last kiss!
FIFTH HUSBAND: And has it come to this?
So help me God, dear Alison,
I'll never strike you. For this thing I've done
You are to blame. Forgive me, I implore.
WIFE OF BATH: Take that to level up the score! (*Hits him.*)
Thus far I am avenged, you thief.
I cannot speak. Now I shall die for grief.
FIFTH HUSBAND: My dear, my own true wife,
Do as you will as long as you have life;
Preserve your honor and keep my estate.
WIFE OF BATH: From that day on we had settled our debate.
I was as kind, God help me, day and dark
As any wife from India to Denmark,
And also true, and so he was to me.
I pray the Lord who sits in majesty
To bless his soul for Christ's own mercy dear.
And now I'll tell my tale, if you will hear.

ALL: By God, madam . . . this is a long preamble to a tale!

WIFE OF BATH: In the old days when King Arthur ruled the nation,
Whom Welshmen speak of with such veneration,
This realm we live in was a fairy land.
The fairy queen danced with her jolly band
On the green meadows where they held dominion.
This was, as I have read, the old opinion;
It chanced that Arthur had a knight who came
Lustily riding home one day from hawking,
And in his path he saw a maiden walking
Before him, stark alone, right in his course.
This young knight took her maidenhead by force.

(SECOND *and* FIFTH PLAYERS *become* TREES, THIRD PLAYER *becomes the* KNIGHT *who rides through woods and pounces on* FOURTH PLAYER. *She struggles briefly and then winds self around him.* FOURTH PLAYER *then becomes the* QUEEN, *climbs ladder down stage left, and uses pillow as crown.* TREES *become* GUARDS.)

QUEEN: King Arthur has given to me, his queen and wife,
The choice to save or kill this handsome knight.
I grant your life, if you can answer me
This question: what is the thing that most of all
Women desire? Think, or your neck will fall
Under the ax! If you cannot let me know
Immediately, I give you leave to go
A twelvemonth and a day, no more, in quest
Of such an answer as will meet the test.
But you must pledge your honor to return
And yield your body, whatever you may learn.

(*Dismisses him.*)

KNIGHT: What can it be that women want the most?

(FOURTH PLAYER *gives the responses as several different people.*)

FOURTH PLAYER: What women want the most is wealth and treasure,
Honor, jollity, and pleasure,
Power,
Sport in bed,
Often to be widowed, often wed.
To a woman's heart what matters

Above all else is to be pleased and flattered.
Men win us best by flattery
And by attention.
Our greatest ease
Is to be free and do just as we please.

KNIGHT: My year is up and now it is the day.

(The WIFE OF BATH *assumes the role of the* OLD WOMAN.)

OLD WOMAN: Sir knight, here runs no thoroughfare.
What are you seeking with such anxious air?
Tell me! The better may your fortune be.
We old folk know a lot of things, you see.

KNIGHT: Good mother, my life's to pay,
That's all too certain, if I cannot say
What women covet most. If you could tell
That secret to me, I'd requite you well.

OLD WOMAN: Give me your hand, and swear me true
That whatsoever I next ask of you,
You'll do it if it lies within your might
And I'll enlighten you before the night.

KNIGHT: Upon my honor, I agree.

OLD WOMAN: Then I dare boast, indeed, I guarantee
Your life is safe. Let me die
If the queen herself won't say the same as I.

(The KNIGHT *helps her onto his pretended horse and they arrive at the court.* SECOND *and* FIFTH PLAYERS *resume* GUARD *positions.)*

KNIGHT: Most of all, my liege and lady,
Women desire to have the sovereignty
And sit in rule and government above
Their husbands, and to have their way in love.
This is what most you want. Spare me or kill
As you may like; I stand here by your will.

QUEEN: That's it!

(She jumps into his arms.)

OLD WOMAN: My sovereign lady queen,
Before your court has risen, do me right!
It was I who taught this answer to the knight,
For which he pledged his honor in my hand,
Solemnly, that the first thing I demand,
He would do it, if it lay within his might.

Before the court I ask you, then, sir knight,
To keep your word and take me as your wife.

(The KNIGHT *falls into faint, caught by* GUARD. *He then goes on his knees.)*

KNIGHT: Alas, old lady,
That was my promise, that I do confess.
For love of God, though, choose a new request!
Take all my wealth, and let my body be.

(The OLD WOMAN *refuses, the* QUEEN *marries them, the* GUARDS *keeping him there. Then the* SECOND, THIRD, *and* FIFTH PLAYERS *become the headboard of a bed, kneeling and using pillows before their faces. The* KNIGHT *avoids entering the bed.)*

OLD WOMAN: Is every knight so backward with a spouse?
Is it a law in Arthur's house?
I am your love, your own, your wedded wife.
You must be mad, the way that you behave!
Tell me my fault, and as God's love can save,
I will amend it, truly, if I can.

(He climbs in bed but puts pillows between them.)

KNIGHT: Amend it?
It can never be amended, truth to tell.
You are so loathsome and so old as well,
And your low birth besides is such a cross
It is no wonder that I turn and toss.
God take my woeful spirit from my breast!
OLD WOMAN: Is this, my dear, the cause of your unrest?
KNIGHT: And do you wonder! Yes, it truly is.
OLD WOMAN: Now, sir, I could amend all this
Within three days, if it should please me to,
And if you deal with me as you should do.
Choose now, which of two courses you will try:
To have me old and ugly till I die
But evermore your true and humble wife,
Never displeasing you in all my life,
Or will you have me rather young and fair
And take your chances on who may repair
To your own house and that because of me
Or to some other place, it well may be.
Now make your choice, whichever you prefer.

KNIGHT: My love and lady, my dear wife,
In your wise government I put my life.
Choose for yourself which course will best agree
With pleasure and honor, both for you and me.
I do not care, choose either of the two;
I am content, whatever pleases you.

OLD WOMAN: Then have I won from you the sovereignty?
Lift up the curtain, see what you may see.
Kiss me, my love. Now we are done with strife,
For on my word, I will be both to you,
That is to say, fair, yes, and faithful too.
May I die mad unless I am as true
As ever wife was since the world was new.

(The KNIGHT *throws away pillows he has grabbed from* PLAYERS *as bed to protect himself from his wife. They had assumed hear no evil, see no evil, speak no evil poses. The* KNIGHT *sees* OLD LADY *as young and beautiful and throws self on her. The* OTHER PLAYERS *all jump on them and the* WIFE OF BATH *emerges from the pile to say the following.)*

WIFE OF BATH: And so they lived in full joy to the end.
And now to all us women may Christ send
Submissive husbands, full of youth in bed,
And grace to outlive all the men we wed.
And I pray Jesus to cut short the lives
Of those who won't be governed by their wives;
And old, ill-tempered niggards who hate expense,
God promptly bring them down with pestilence!

(The PLAYERS, *all but the* FIFTH ONE, *become* PILGRIMS *and ride off into the audience. The* FIFTH PLAYER *plays the recorder, then notices they are gone, and follows.)*

INTERMISSION

PART II

The PLAYERS *ride onto the stage from the audience,* FIFTH PLAYER *playing recorder—riding music.* CHAUCER *takes quilt used in previous scenes, reverses it to purple side, and puts it on* FIFTH PLAYER, *who wears it as a cloak and becomes the* PARDONER.

CHAUCER: Now my fine friend, you Pardoner,
Be quick, tell us a tale of mirth or fun.

(*The* PLAYERS *arrange two ladders on their sides as a table and sit around it to drink. The* PARDONER *drinks from a long pillow representing a bottle.*)

PARDONER: By St. Ninian, it shall be done,
But at this tavern here, before my tale,
I'll just go in and have some bread and ale.
PRIORESS: Speak no ribaldry!
Tell us a moral tale, one to make clear
Some lesson to us, and we'll gladly hear.
PARDONER: Just as you wish, but I must think
Of something edifying while I drink.

(*The* PARDONER *picks up pillows as he discourses to represent bulls, relics, etc.*)

In churches, when I preach,
I use, milords, a lofty style of speech
And ring it out as roundly as a bell,
Knowing by rote all that I have to tell.
My text is ever the same, and ever was:
Radix malorum est cupiditas.
First I inform them whence I come; that done,
I then display my papal bulls, each one.
I show my license first, my body's warrant,
Sealed by the bishop, for it would be abhorrent
If any man made bold, though priest or clerk,
To interrupt me in Christ's holy work.
And after that I give myself full scope.
Bulls in the name of cardinal and pope,
Of bishops and of patriarchs I show.
I say in Latin some few words or so
To spice my sermon, it flavors my appeal
And stirs my listeners to greater zeal.
Then I display my cases made of glass
Crammed to the top with rags and bones. They pass
For relics with all the people in the place.
I have a shoulder bone in a metal case,

Part of a sheep owned by a holy Jew.
"Good men," I say, "heed what I'm telling you:
Just let this bone be dipped in any well
And if cow, calf, or sheep, or ox should swell
From eating a worm, or by a worm be stung,
Take water from this well and wash its tongue
And it is healed at once. And furthermore
    This bone cures jealousies galore.
Though into a jealous madness a man fell,
Let him cook his soup in water from this well,
He'll never, though for truth he knew her sin,
Suspect his wife again, though she took in
A priest, or even two of them or three.

(*He addresses audience.*)

    "There is one word of warning I must say,
Good men and women. If any here today
Has done a sin so horrible to name
He daren't be shriven of it for the shame,
Or if any woman, young or old, is here
Who has cuckolded her husband, be it clear
They may not make an offering in that case
To these my relics; they have no power nor grace.
But any who is free of such dire blame,
Let him come up and offer in God's name
And I'll absolve him through the authority
That by the pope's bull has been granted me."
    By such hornswoggling I've won, year by year,
A hundred marks since being a pardoner.

(*Climbs tall ladder stage left.*)

I stand in my pulpit like a true divine,
And when the people sit I preach my line
To ignorant souls, as you have heard before,
And tell skullduggeries by the hundred more.
Then I take care to stretch my neck well out
And over the people I nod and peer about
Just like a pigeon perching on a shed.
My hands fly and my tongue wags in my head
So busily that to watch me is a joy.
Avarice is the theme that I employ

In all my sermons, to make the people free
In giving pennies—especially to me.
My mind is fixed on what I stand to win
And not at all upon correcting sin.
I do not care, when they are in the grave,
If souls go berry-picking that I could save.
    But to put my purpose briefly, I confess
I preach for nothing but for covetousness.
That's why my text is still and ever was
Radix malorum est cupiditas.
For by this text I can denounce, indeed,
The very vice I practice, which is greed.
But though that sin is lodged in my own heart,
I am able to make other people part
From avarice, and sorely to repent,
Though that is not my principal intent.

(*Descends ladder.*)

But in conclusion, lords, I will get down
To business: you would have me tell a tale.
Now that I've had a drink of corny ale,
By God, I hope the thing I'm going to tell
Is one that you'll have reason to like well.
For though myself a very sinful man,
I can tell a moral tale, indeed I can,
One that I use to bring the profits in
While preaching. Now be still, and I'll begin.

(SECOND *and* FOURTH PLAYERS *gamble with pillows as dice:* THIRD PLAYER *plays guitar and* FIRST PLAYER *serves drinks.*)

There was a company of young folk living
One time in Flanders, who were bent on giving
Their lives to follies and extravagances,
Brothels and taverns, where they held their dances
With lutes, harps, and guitars, diced at all hours,
And also ate and drank beyond their powers,
Through which they paid the devil sacrifice
In the devil's temple with their drink and dice.

(*The guitar music changes to a funeral lament—all* PLAYERS *watch as if coffin is going by.* FIRST PLAYER *becomes a* SERVANT, SECOND PLAYER RIOTER ONE, THIRD PLAYER RIOTER TWO, *and* FOURTH PLAYER, RIOTER THREE.)

RIOTER ONE: Go out and try
To learn whose corpse is being carried by.
Get me his name, and get it right. Take heed.
SERVANT: Sir, there isn't any need.
I learned before you came here, by two hours.
He was, it happens, an old friend of yours,
And all at once, there on his bench upright
As he was sitting drunk, he was killed last night.
A sly thief, Death men call him, who deprives
All the people in this country of their lives,
Came with his spear and smiting his heart in two
Went on his business with no more ado.
A thousand have been slaughtered by his hand
During this plague. And, sir, before you stand
Within his presence, it should be necessary,
It seems to me, to know your adversary.
Be evermore prepared to meet this foe.
My mother taught me thus; that's all I know.

(SERVANT *and* PARDONER *rearrange table ladders as tree upstage left—one on top of the other upside down.*)

RIOTER TWO: Is it so dangerous with this thief to meet?
I'll look for him by every path and street,
I vow it, by God's holy bones! Hear me,
Fellows of mine, we are all one, we three.
Let each of us hold up his hand to the other
And each of us become his fellow's brother.
We'll slay this Death, who slaughters and betrays.
He shall be slain whose hand so many slays.

(*The* PARDONER, *who has added a hood to his cloak to become* OLD MAN *now moves in close behind them—he touches* RIOTER ONE *and plays dance of death music on recorder, leading the* THREE *in a dance of death.*)

OLD MAN: God bless you, lords, and be your guide.
RIOTER TWO: Old beggar, I hope you meet with evil grace!
Why are you all wrapped up except your face?
What are you doing alive so many a year?
OLD MAN: Because I can,
Though I should walk to India, find no man
In any village or any town,

Who for my age is willing to lay down
His youth. So I must keep my old age still
For as long a time as it may be God's will.
Nor will Death take my life from me, alas!
Thus like a restless prisoner I pass
And on the ground, which is my mother's gate,
I walk and with my staff both early and late
I knock and say, "Dear mother, let me in!
See how I vanish, flesh, and blood, and skin!
Alas, when shall my bones be laid to rest?
I would exchange with you my clothing chest,
Mother, that in my chamber long has been
For an old haircloth rag to wrap me in."
And yet she still refuses me that grace.
All white, therefore, and withered is my face.
But sirs, you do yourselves no courtesy
To speak to an old man so churlishly
Unless he had wronged you either in word or deed.
As you yourselves in Holy Writ may read,
"Before an aged man whose head is hoar
Men ought to rise." I counsel you, therefore,
No harm nor wrong here to an old man do,
No more than you would have men do to you
In your old age, if you so long abide.
And God be with you, whether you walk or ride!
I must go yonder where I have to go.

RIOTER ONE: No, you old beggar, by St. John, not so,
As for me,
By God, you won't get off so easily!
You spoke just now of that false traitor, Death,
Who in this land robs all our friends of breath.
Tell where he is, since you must be his spy,
Or you will suffer for it, so say I
By God and by the holy sacrament.
You are in league with him, false thief, and bent
On killing us young folk, that's clear to my mind.

OLD MAN: If you are so impatient, sirs, to find
Death, turn up this crooked way,
For in that grove I left him, truth to say,
Beneath a tree, and there he will abide.

No boast of yours will make him run and hide.
Do you see that oak tree? Just there you will find
This Death, and God, who bought again mankind,
Save and amend you!

(OLD MAN *goes to tree, climbs one step of ladder and plays "Dance of Death" music. The* THREE RIOTERS *do a dance of death until they arrive at the tree.* OLD MAN *throws down bright colored ribbons which they take as gold.*)

RIOTER TWO: Brothers, listen to what I say.
My head is sharp, for all I joke and play.
Fortune has given us this pile of treasure
To set us up in lives of ease and pleasure.
RIOTER ONE: Lightly it comes, lightly we'll make it go.
RIOTER THREE: God's precious dignity! Who was to know
We'd ever tumble on such luck today?
RIOTER TWO: If we could only carry this gold away,
Home to my house, or either one of yours—
For well you know that all this gold is ours—
We'd touch the summit of felicity.
But still, by daylight that can hardly be.
People would call us thieves, too bold for stealth,
And they would have us hanged for our own wealth.
RIOTER ONE: It must be done by night, that's our best plan,
As prudently and slyly as we can.
RIOTER TWO: Hence my proposal is that we should all
Draw lots, and let's see where the lot will fall,
And the one of us draws the shortest stick
Shall run back to the town, and make it quick,
And bring us bread and wine here on the sly,
And two of us will keep a watchful eye
Over this gold; and if he doesn't stay
Too long in town, we'll carry this gold away
By night, wherever we all agree it's best.

(*They draw lots;* RIOTER THREE *wins and goes off running in place stage right.*)

You know that by sworn oath you are my brother
I'll tell you something you can profit by.
Our friend has gone, that's clear to any eye,
And here is gold, abundant as can be,

That we propose to share alike, we three.
But if I worked it out, as I could do,
So that it could be shared between us two,
Wouldn't that be a favor, a friendly one?

RIOTER ONE: How can that be done,
I don't quite see. He knows we have the gold.
What shall we do, or what shall he be told?

RIOTER TWO: Will you keep the secret tucked inside your head?
And in a few words
I'll tell you how to bring this end about.

RIOTER ONE: Granted, never doubt,
I won't betray you, that you can believe.

RIOTER TWO: Now, we are two, as you perceive,
And two of us must have more strength than one.
When he sits down, get up as if in fun
And wrestle with him. While you play this game
I'll run him through the ribs. You do the same
With your dagger there, and then this gold shall be
Divided, dear friend, between you and me.
Then all that we desire we can fulfill,
And both of us can roll the dice at will.

(RIOTERS ONE *and* TWO *freeze.* RIOTER THREE *approaches ladder stage left where* FIRST PLAYER *becomes* APOTHECARY.)

RIOTER THREE: O Lord, were there some way I might
Have all this treasure to myself alone,
There isn't a man who dwells beneath God's throne
Could live a life as merry as mine should be!
(*To* APOTHECARY.) Give me some poison if you will to free
Me from some rats. I've had my fill
Of capon-killing pole cats too and will
Get my revenge on vermin that devour
Me through the long night hours.

APOTHECARY: You shall have
A drug that as I hope the Lord will save
My soul, no living thing in all creation,
Eating or drinking of this preparation
A dose no bigger than a grain of wheat,
But promptly with his death-stroke he shall meet.
Die, that he will, and in a briefer while

Than you can walk the distance of a mile,
This poison is so strong and virulent.

(RIOTER THREE *takes back bottles [pillows] and gives them to others, who carry out their plan in pantomime, kill him, drink, and die. The* OLD MAN *comes out, closes their eyes, throws off hood; others all return to* PILGRIM *roles.*)

PARDONER: —Sirs, thus I preach. And now
Christ Jesus, our souls' healer, show you how
Within his pardon evermore to rest,
For that, I will not lie to you, is best.
But in my tale, sirs, I forgot one thing.
The relics and the pardons that I bring
Here in my pouch, no man in the whole land
Has finer, given me by the pope's own hand.
If any of you devoutly wants to offer
And have my absolution, come and proffer
Whatever you have to give. Kneel down right here,
Humbly, and take my pardon, full and clear,
Or have a new, fresh pardon if you like
At the end of every mile of road we strike,
As long as you keep offering ever newly
Good coins, not counterfeit, but minted truly.
Indeed it is an honor I confer
On each of you, an authentic pardoner
Going along to absolve you as you ride.
For in the country mishaps may betide—
One or another of you in due course
May break his neck by falling from his horse.
Think what security it gives you all
That in this company I chanced to fall
Who can absolve you each, both low and high,
When the soul, alas, shall from the body fly!

(*Addressing* THIRD PLAYER *who resumes role of* HOST.)

And I advise my friend here to begin
For he's the man enveloped most by sin.
Come, you may offer first, and once that's done,
Then you shall kiss the relics, every one,
Yes, for a penny! Come, undo your purse!

HOST: Oh no I won't, for I should have Christ's curse!
I'll nothing of the sort, for love or riches!

You'd make me kiss a piece of your old britches
And for a saintly relic make it pass
Although it had the tincture of your ass.

CHAUCER: No more,
This has gone far enough. Now as before,
Sir Pardoner, be gay, look cheerfully,
And you, Sir Host, who are so dear to me,
Come, kiss the Pardoner, I beg of you,
And Pardoner, draw near, and let us do
As we've been doing, let us laugh and play.
Now kiss, and we'll continue on our way.

(*The* PARDONER *holds out hand and the* HOST *kisses his ring, then rides off rubbing his lips with repugnance. The* PARDONER *removes cloak to resume* PILGRIM *role. The* PILGRIMS *all ride during the following exchange.*

CHAUCER: Come over here,
You priest, come hither, you Sir John, draw near!
Tell us a thing to make our spirits glad.
Be cheerful, though the jade you ride is bad.
What if your horse is miserable and lean?
If he will carry you, don't care a bean!
Keep up a joyful heart, and look alive.

NUN'S PRIEST: Yes, sir, and as I hope to thrive,
If I weren't merry, I know I'd get reproach
So with no more ado my tale I'll broach.

(PLAYERS *arrange ladders so that one is upstage center, one is downstage left, and one remains upstage left.*)

NUN'S PRIEST: Once a poor widow, aging year by year,
Lived in a tiny cottage that stood near
A clump of shade trees rising in a dale.

(*The* NUN'S PRIEST *creates* WIDOW *played by* THIRD PLAYER *while the* FIRST, SECOND, *and* FIFTH PLAYERS *become* BARNYARD ANIMALS. *The* WIDOW *leads them about, feeds them, milks* COW, *etc.*)

This widow, of whom I tell you in my tale,
Since the last day that she had been a wife
Had led a very patient, simple life.
She had but few possessions to content her.
By thrift and husbandry of what God sent her
She and two daughters found the means to dine.

She had no more than three well-fattened swine,
As many cows, and one sheep, Moll by name.
Her bower and hall were black from the hearth-flame
Where she had eaten many a slender meal.
No dainty morsel did her palate feel
And no sharp sauce was needed with her pottage.
Her table was in keeping with her cottage.
Excess had never given her disquiet.
Her only doctor was a moderate diet,
And exercise, and a heart that was contented.
If she did not dance, at least no gout prevented;
No apoplexy had destroyed her head.
She never drank wine, whether white or red.
She served brown bread and milk, loaves white or black,
Singed bacon, all this with no sense of lack,
And now and then an egg or two. In short,
She was a dairy woman of a sort.
She had a yard, on the inside fenced about
With hedges, and an empty ditch without,
In which she kept a cock, called Chanticleer.

(SECOND PLAYER *crawls through* NUN'S PRIEST'S *legs and is "born."*)

In all the realm of crowing he'd no peer.
WIDOW: His comb, like a crenelated castle wall,
Red as fine coral, stood up proud and tall.
His bill was black; like polished jet it glowed,
And he was azure-legged and azure-toed.
As lilies were his nails, they were so white;
Like burnished gold his hue, it shone so bright.
NUN'S PRIEST: This cock had in his princely sway and measure
Seven hens to satisfy his every pleasure,
Who were his sisters and his sweethearts true,
Each wonderfully like him in her hue,
Of whom the fairest-feathered throat to see
Was fair Dame Partlet.

(FIRST PLAYER *crawls through* NUN'S PRIEST'S *legs and is "born."*)

Courteous was she,
Discreet, and always acted debonairly.
She was sociable, and bore herself so fairly,
Since the very time that she was seven nights old,

The heart of Chanticleer was in her hold
As if she had him locked up, every limb.
He loved her so that all was well with him.

(*They dance ballet together.*)

It was a joy, when the sun would spring,
To hear them both together sweetly sing,
"My love has gone to the country, far away!"

(*They sing duet.*)

For as I understand it, in that day
The animals and birds could speak and sing.
Now on one day when morn began to spring,
When Chanticleer sat on his perch and next
Him sat Dame Partlet, he was sorely vext
And groaned like someone having dreadful dreams;

DAME PARTLET: Soul of my passion,
What ails you that you groan in such a fashion?
You are always a sound sleeper. Fie, for shame!

CHANTICLEER: Dame,
Take no offense, I beg you, on this score.
I dreamt, by God, I was in a plight so sore
Just now, my heart still quivers from the fright.
Now God see that my dream turns out all right
And keep my flesh and body from foul seizure!
I dreamed I was strutting in our yard at leisure
When there I saw, among the weeds and vines,
A beast, he was like a hound, and had designs
Upon my person, and would have killed me dead.
His coat was not quite yellow, not quite red,
And both his ears and tail were tipped with black
Unlike the fur along his sides and back.
He had a small snout and a fiery eye.
His look for fear still makes me almost die.
And this it is that made me groan and start.

DAME PARTLET: For shame! Fie on you, faint heart!
Alas, alas, and by great God above,
Now you have lost my heart and all my love!
I cannot love a coward, as I'm blest!
Whatever any woman may protest,
We all want, could it be so, for a start,

Husbands who are wise and stout of heart,
Alas, and can a nightmare set you screaming?
God knows there's only vanity in dreaming!
Dreams are produced by such unseemly capers
As overeating; they come from stomach vapors
When a man's humors aren't behaving right
From some excess. This dream you had tonight,
It comes straight from the superfluity
Of your red choler, certain as can be,
Cato, that has been thought so wise a man,
Didn't he tell us, "Put no stock in dreams"?
Now, sir, when we fly from our beams,
For God's sake, go and take a laxative!
On my salvation, as I hope to live,
I give you good advice, and no mere folly:
Purge both your choler and your melancholy!
You musn't wait or let yourself bog down,
And since there is no druggist in this town
I shall myself prescribe for what disturbs
Your humors, and instruct you in the herbs
That will be good for you. For I shall find
Here in our yard herbs of the proper kind
For purging you both under and above.

CHANTICLEER: Madame, thanks for all your lore.
But still, to speak of Cato, though his name
For wisdom has enjoyed so great a fame,
And though he counseled us there was no need
To be afraid of dreams, by God, men read
Of many a man of more authority
Than this Don Cato could pretend to be
Who in old books declare the opposite,
And by experience they have settled it,
That dreams are omens and prefigurations
Both of good fortune and tribulations
That life and its vicissitudes present.
This question leaves no room for argument.
Think of the king of Egypt, Don Pharaoh;
Of his butler and his baker think also,
Whether they found that dreams have no result.
Whoever will search through kingdoms and consult

Their histories reads many a wondrous thing
Of dreams. What about Croesus, Lydian king—
Didn't he dream he was sitting on a tree,
Which meant he would be hanged? Andromache,
The woman who was once great Hector's wife,
On the day that Hector was to lose his life,
The very night before his blood was spilled
She dreamed of how her husband would be killed
If he went out to battle on that day.
She warned him; but he would not heed nor stay.
In spite of her he rode out on the plain,
And by Achilles he was promptly slain.
But all that story is too long to tell,
And it is nearly day. I must not dwell
Upon this matter. Briefly, in conclusion,
I say this dream will bring me to confusion
And mischief of some sort. And furthermore,
On laxatives, I say, I set no store,
For they are poisonous, I'm sure of it.
I do not trust them! I like them not one bit!
Now let's talk cheerfully, and forget all this.
My pretty Partlet, by my hope of bliss,
In one thing God has sent me ample grace,
For when I see the beauty of your face,
You are so scarlet-red about the eye,
It is enough to make my terrors die.
For just as true as *In principio*
Mulier est hominis confusio—
And Madame, what this Latin means is this:
"Woman is man's whole comfort and true bliss"—
When I feel you soft at night, and I beside you,
Although it's true, alas, I cannot ride you
Because our perch is built so narrowly,
I am then so full of pure felicity
That I defy whatever sort of dream!

NUN'S PRIEST: And day being come, he flew down from the beam
He was a prince, his fears were gone it seems.
The morning had not passed the hour of prime
When he treaded Partlet for the twentieth time.

Grim as a lion he strolled to and fro,
And strutted only on his either toe.

CHANTICLEER: Partlet, my world's delight,
Hear all these birds, how happily they sing,
And see the pretty flowers, how they spring.
With solace and with joy my spirits dance!

NUN'S PRIEST: But suddenly he met a sore mischance,
For in the end joys ever turn to woes.

(FIFTH PLAYER *as* FOX *comes under* NUN'S PRIEST'S *legs and is "born."*)

A sly iniquitous fox, with black-tipped ears,
Who had lived in the neighboring wood for some three years,
His fated fancy swollen to a height,
Had broken through the hedges that same night
Into the yard where in his pride sublime
Chanticleer with his seven wives passed the time.
Quietly in a bed of herbs he lay
Till it was past the middle of the day,
Waiting his hour on Chanticleer to fall
As gladly do these murderers, one and all,
Who lie in wait, concealed, to murder men.
O murderer, lurking traitorous in your den!
O new Iscariot, second Ganelon,
False hypocrite, Greek Sinon, who brought on
The utter woe of Troy and all her sorrow!
O Chanticleer, accursed be that morrow
When to the yard you flew down from the beams!
That day, as you were well warned in your dreams,
Would threaten you with dire catastrophe.
Women have many times, as wise men hold,
Offered advice that left men in the cold.
A woman's counsel brought us first to woe
And out of Paradise made Adam go
Where he lived a merry life and one of ease.
But since I don't know whom I may displease
By giving women's words an ill report,
Pass over it; I only spoke in sport.
There are books about it you can read or skim in,
And you'll discover what they say of women.

I'm telling you the cock's words, and not mine.
Harm in no woman at all can I divine.

(*The* FOX *approaches* CHANTICLEER *who hides under ladder upstage center.*)

FOX: Where are you going, kind sir?
Are you afraid of me, who am your friend?
Truly, I'd be a devil from end to end
If I meant you any harm or villainy.
I have not come to invade your privacy.
In truth, the only reason that could bring
This visit of mine was just to hear you sing.
Beyond a doubt, you have as fine a voice
As any angel who makes heaven rejoice.
Also you have more feeling in your note
Than Boëthius, or any tuneful throat.
Milord your father once—and may God bless
His soul—your noble mother too, no less,
Have been inside my house, to my great ease.
And verily sir, I should be glad to please
You also. But for singing, I declare
As I enjoy my eyes, that precious pair,
Save you, I never heard a man so sing
As your father did when night was on the wing.

(CHANTICLEER *emerges and begins to preen and strut.*)

Straight from the heart, in truth, came all his song,
And to make his voice more resonant and strong
He would strain until he shut his either eye,
So loud and lordly would he make his cry,
And stand up on his tiptoes therewithal
And stretch his neck till it grew long and small.
Sing, sir! Show me, for holy charity,
Can you imitate your father, that wise man?

(CHANTICLEER *sings "My Love Is Far From Land" with elbows out. The* FOX *attempts to lock elbows with him when he isn't looking and succeeds on the third try. Elbows locked, they move about back to back.*)

NUN'S PRIEST: In truth, no lamentation ever rose,
No shriek of ladies when before its foes
Ilium fell, and Pyrrhus with drawn blade

Had seized King Priam by the beard and made
An end of him—the *Aeneid* tells the tale—
Such as the hens made with their piteous wail
In their enclosure, seeing the dread sight
Of Chanticleer.

WIDOW: Help, help! Alas! Alack!
The fox, the fox!

(*Then all repeat it and join in a chase.*)

CHANTICLEER: God be my help, sir, but I'd tell them all,
That is, if I were you, "Plague on you fall!
Go back, proud fools! Now that I've reached the wood,
I'll eat the cock at once, for all the good
Your noise can do. Here Chanticleer shall stay."

FOX: Fine! I'll do just what you say.

(CHANTICLEER *escapes to ladder upstage left which he climbs.*)

Alas, alas, O Chanticleer!
In as much as I have given you cause to fear
By seizing you and bearing you away,
I have done you wrong, I am prepared to say.
But, sir, I did it with no ill intent.
Come down, and I shall tell you what I meant.
So help me God, it's truth I'll offer you!

CHANTICLEER: No, no, We're both fools, through and through.
But curse my blood and bones for the chief dunce
If you deceive me oftener than once!
You shall never again by flattery persuade me
To sing and wink my eyes, by him that made me.
For he that willfully winks when he should see,
God never bless him with prosperity!

FOX: Ah, with mischief may God greet
The man ungoverned, rash, and indiscreet
Who babbles when to hold his tongue were needful!

NUN'S PRIEST: Such is it to be reckless and unheedful
And trust in flattery. But you who hold
That this is a mere trifle I have told,
Concerning only a fox, or a cock and hen,
Think twice, and take the moral, my good men!
For truly, of whatever is written, all
Is written for our doctrine, says St. Paul.

Then take the fruit, and let the chaff lie still.
Now, gracious God, if it should be your will,
As my Lord teaches, make us all good men
And bring us to your holy bliss! Amen.

(*As* CHAUCER *comes forward to make his retraction, the* OTHER PLAYERS *repeat highlights of the program in slow motion—such as the window scene from "The Miller's Tale" and the bed scene in "The Wife of Bath's Tale"*).

CHAUCER: Now pray I to all those who hear this little treatise that if there be anything in it that pleases them, that they thank our Lord Jesus Christ for it, from whom proceeds all wit and all goodness. And if there be anything that displeases them, I pray them also that they attribute it to my want of skill, and not to my purpose, which would gladly have said better if I had had skill. For our book says, "All that is written is written for our doctrine," and that is my intent. Wherefore I beseech you humbly, for the mercy of God, that you pray for me that Christ have mercy on me and forgive me my sins; and especially for my translations and writings that concern worldly vanities, which I renounce in my retractations; such as the tales of Canterbury, those that make for sin. Grant me the grace of true penitence, confession, and satisfaction to perform in this present life, through the benign grace of him that is king of kings and priest over all priests, that bought us with the precious blood of his heart; so that I may be one of them at the day of doom that shall be saved.

(*As* CHAUCER *completes the retraction, the* OTHER PLAYERS *are piled up in bed as they were in "The Wife of Bath's Tale" at the end of PART I. They beckon to* CHAUCER *to join them as he comes to the end and on his "Amen" they all point at him, jump up, grab him, and carry him out through the audience, yelping with glee as they did when they entered.*)

THE END

APPENDIX:

The Student as Artist

A CANTERBURY CAPER IN CALIFORNIA
by Grant McKernie

As a member of THE COLLECTION, and a teacher as well as a performer in the group's summer workshop on The Role of Dramatic Performance in Education, I became convinced that other groups besides teachers could organize and utilize the ideas and techniques of our group of teacher/artists. Because I believed that students could benefit from participation in such a group, I embarked on an experiment at San José State University in San José, California that specifically involved the student as artist.

Initiated in the spring of 1973, the two-part project used students in an advanced acting class and those in a dramatic literature class (Modern European Drama). The acting students were cast in *Shakespeare's Mirror* and *A Canterbury Caper* and began rehearsals immediately. They rehearsed six hours a week for seven weeks before their first performances. The literature class was conducted as usual except that the students' term project was to write a "COLLECTION-styled" script on one of the playwrights discussed in the course. None of the students was in both projects, although such an alternative arrangement could be desirable.

The goals of the two groups were different. The purposes of the acting project were: to involve the students in a script which provided each actor with a number of roles, the opportunity to change character within the same performance thereby increasing versatility; to provide students with the opportunity to play directly to an audience as narrator or storyteller as well as character; and to enhance the students' awareness of the range and scope of the authors involved (Shakespeare and Chaucer). The purposes of the script-writing project were: to increase the literature students' understanding of and involvement with one playwright; to help them discover and articulate the central characteristics and themes of the playwright; to make them aware of the theatrical potential of the material they had been reading; to get them to think in the dramatic medium by asking them to find a central dramatic metaphor which captured the ideas of one playwright; and to have them develop their own narrative, explaining the playwright as they understood him in a dramatic context rather than in a research paper.

Because *Shakespeare's Mirror* was directed by another faculty member, it will not be treated here except to note that the script was modified and altered to fit the particular actors involved. That is, a few Shakespearean scenes other than those in the script were used because they better suited the talents of the particular cast. Specifically, the Juliet-Nurse scene (Act II, scene V) substituted for the Juliet soliloquy, both to take advantage of an older woman in the group who could play the Nurse well and to counter the fact that there was no one quite strong enough to do the soliloquy. A second change involved the addition of the Hamlet-Laertes duel in Act V to capitalize on the fencing skills of two of the actors. These modifications point up a central advantage of the script idea, *viz.*, its flexibility and adaptability. Not only is it flexible in terms of length and presentational components, but it is adaptable to the group of actors selected for performance. By maintaining the central metaphor and the major narration, the revised script held to the original intent with remarkable ease and success.

Two major problems arose during work on the Chaucer script. The first was the students' lack of knowledge about Chaucer. Three of the five had read only the Prologue and one or two of the tales in high school. Consequently, they tended to treat each scene in the script as a play, bringing little external information to bear on the shape of the whole piece and failing to relate each individual story to the others. More specifically, they made no connection between the tale and the character telling the story, thus missing much of the dramatic richness of Chaucer's commentary. As a consequence, we had to spend a considerable amount of time talking about the tales, their origin and development, and their interrelationships. Information about Chaucer's life was also pertinent, and it became crucial above all to give the actors a sense of the medieval period. "The Pardoner's Tale," for example, is a light and fairly harmless tale of youthful bravado until it is placed in its appropriate historical context. Both the sinister and mystical qualities of the story come alive when the actors have a feel for the historical realities which lie behind the story. The characterization of the Pardoner himself may be deepened if one shifts from a dottore-like Elmer Gantry to a partially malevolent and thoroughly hypocritical individual similar to actual pardoners of Chaucer's day.

The script, however, does not simply provide a pretext for discussing literary history; it becomes a vehicle for realizing the significance and consequences of that history. It brings alive not only the material, but the author and his times and society. Through the subtlety of line readings, gestures, and stage movements, the many levels of meaning in the *Tales* may be conveyed to an audience, but these meanings must first be understood by the student actors.

The second major problem for the students was the format of the script which requires a presentational style, meaning simply that the actor often presents the material to the audience rather than representing a character on stage as if the audience were not there (See p. xv). Most actors in the United States are accustomed to the representational style of performing as if the situation were real and as if a "fourth wall" existed between them and the audience. They relate to the other characters as their own character, but they do not relate to the audience either as character or as actor. The Shakespeare script, however, calls for the actors to address the audience directly as themselves in the narration and as the characters in the scenes, while the Chaucer script calls for them to address the audience directly as characters telling a story as well as characters in a story. For many of our acting students, this interaction with the audience presented a formidable challenge. One actor, when asked to talk directly to the audience, stuttered and stammered as if asked to disrobe. Despite numerous exercises and discussion this fear was never completely overcome until performance. Once he realized that the audience enjoyed such direct contact he relaxed; in fact he created new levels of energy previously not used in rehearsal, as did the others. It is indeed difficult for an actor to feel comfortable with the presentational style in rehearsal because it is completely dependent on an audience for its proper effect. Once the audience is there, however, its purpose and rewards become self-evident.

Apart from the obvious educational values of the script which were realized by the performers and the audience, e.g., knowledge of Chaucer and his time period, appreciation of a different dramatic form, realization of the dramatic quality of the *Tales* themselves, the students made other discoveries as a consequence of performing the script. They became very aware, for example, of the humanity that exists within each of the characters in the *Tales.* As one student reported, "I always thought that the characters of a story were just that: characters of a story. It never occurred to me that they could have the same vitality as the characters of a play." The first part of that quotation reveals a misconception about fictional characters; namely, that they do not have the individuality that acting students associate with the characters of plays. It was easy to discover motivations, strategies, and superobjectives for each character once the students realized the characters could be developed for a stage presentation. Chaucer's skill is such that there is ample characterization provided for fully developed interpretations. Particularly in performance these interpretations developed a vitality quite equal to the robust and hardy strength with which the literary style of Chaucer is suffused.

In working with both the Shakespeare and Chaucer scripts, we found that neither one required seasoned actors to be appropriately and successfully performed. The Prologue to *A Canterbury Caper,* for instance, is to be spoken in the Middle English of Chaucer's time. In THE COLLECTION'S original production, the lines were spoken beautifully, poetically, and accurately. The characters then ran onstage, and the actress speaking the Prologue leaped into their arms. In our production, the woman reading the Prologue could not master the Middle English; we decided to have her stumble purposefully over the phrases, at first stuttering, then fracturing the pronunciations. Finally, she threw up her arms in despair and leapt willingly into the arms of the jeering characters. In the original production, Chaucer was portrayed as a kindly, warm, and modest person; in our production he was an acerbic, satiric, and keenly perceptive one, a difference due as much to the personality of the actors as to any intentional interpretive differences. The important point is that both characterizations were effective and that the script lends itself to realization by actors with a wide range of performing abilities.

One anecdote deserves mention because it reveals the kinds of discoveries the students were making. The woman playing Pertelote had more difficulty with her role and the entire script than anyone else in the cast. Despite help offered through improvisations and various acting exercises, she simply balked at the whole format. Not until the opening performance did her attitude change from irascibility and indifference to joy and involvement, but it was a year later before I discovered the reason. It was then that she confessed she had hated the script and me at first because I had cast her as a chicken. Now she wanted to thank me because I made her realize that she had a comic quality in her acting which she had not thought was there. Before performing she was not aware of the humanity of the Pertelote character which would enable her to demonstrate her talent, nor was she fully aware of her abilities as an actress. By performing the Chaucer script she realized both of these.

The second part of the student-as-artist project utilized THE COLLECTION'S scripts as a teaching device for learning through writing rather than learning through performing. Each student in the dramatic literature class was asked to write a script similar in format to the Chaucer and Shakespeare scripts with these instructions:

1. Each script should focus on one playwright whose major works should be read by the student who should also read sufficient additional material, such as letters, novels, other plays, and criticism to gain a solid appreciation of the style, technique, and major characteristics of the playwright.

2. Each script should be designed for performance and be roughly forty-five minutes in length. There must be a minimum of three scenes from different plays. The scenes chosen should reflect the basic ideas, technique, and style of the playwright. They should include no more than five people (or at least require no more than five actors) and need minimal staging.

3. The script should contain narrative between the scenes both to explain the playwright's style in the particular scene and

to give appropriate background necessary to an appreciation of the scene. The narrative should be dramatically interesting and as brief as possible. Narratives which include stage business are preferable.

4. Each script should be organized around a central dramatic or theatrical metaphor which illustrates and captures the essence of the playwright from the student's point of view, and helps to unite the narration and the scenes.

The educational possibilities in requiring such a writing assignment are many. It encourages close study of the technique and style of the playwright without requiring extended articulation about them (though this can be a requisite goal in some classes). It encourages students to study scenes for their dramatic and performance values, such as continuity, consistency, and development, as well as for their place in the playwright's *oeuvre*. It enables students to think of the potential of the dramatic medium and to work with that medium in their own minds to test what will work with an audience and what won't. Finally, writing the narration requires them to make succinct statements of their attitudes toward the playwright.

The search for a central metaphor which captures the essence of the playwright also proved to have both delightful and informative consequences. The students spent hours talking with each other and with me searching for one overriding theme or idea within the playwright's material which could be visualized theatrically. The concept of visualization was initially difficult for the students, but it proved truly exciting once they began to realize its purpose and potential. One student working with Arthur Schnitzler decided that contemporary Vienna was the appropriate setting for her play, and she set the script in a Viennese coffeehouse with the playwright writing sketches at a table to one side of the stage. This was remarkably similar to the format later used by a PBS series on Schnitzler's short stories. Another student had three couples in period costumes waltzing around the stage during the narration; when the music stopped, two couples would freeze in position while the third would step forward and perform a scene from Schnitzler's work.

The independent work of three students studying the Italian playwright Pirandello demonstrates that there is no single correct metaphor for each playwright and that each one selected has unique advantages. A central theme in Pirandello's work is the confusion of truth and illusion, and his major plays frequently involve characters who are not what they appear to be. In *Six Characters in Search of an Author,* for example, we are never certain whether a stage murder at the end of the play is part of the play, part of the past history of the characters, or part of reality which has intruded onto the stage. One student envisioned her script in front of a stage of mirrors so that the audience could always see itself onstage and the characters would always have a double image in everything they did. At the end the characters walked into the mirrors, leaving the audience to stare at themselves. A second script involved filming the entire script and then showing it on a large screen at the same time that the same script was performed live. The idea was to make the film characters' actors look more lifelike than the live performers. The script ended with the stage actors killing themselves while the film actors laughed at them. The third script used the character Henry IV from the Pirandello play of that name. In the play Henry is a twentieth-century individual pretending to be an aging eleventh-century German monarch who is pretending to be himself at a younger age. In using him as narrator, the script added yet another dimension to that of the character; he is also a narrator pretending to be a twentieth-century individual pretending to be . . . .

After initial unease because of the unfamiliarity of the idea, students responded most positively to the development of their scripts. The combination of reading more plays by a playwright of their choosing and using their imagination to put together their scripts proved enjoyable and valuable. Although only one of the scripts was performed in its entirety, educational values of the script-writing process were realized in the classroom. Students felt that the playwrights they studied were "their" playwrights. They spoke more freely in class discussions on their playwright. They understood how a critic develops an understanding of a playwright's style. And they could better analyze other playwrights for their theatrical potential.

The major of the students did not seem to be a factor in the success of the project. The six theater majors and three English majors did not appear to have any advantage over the students from other fields, nor were their projects better than those of the others. Such script writing also appealed both to students who enjoyed writing papers and to those who didn't; the latter rationalized that the scripts "really" weren't papers.

While the students were preparing their scripts, they were able to see the Shakespeare and Chaucer scripts performed by the acting students. Because the acting and literature classes were working on the same kind of project, it was extremely helpful to the literature students to see what a finished script would look like. This book makes those two scripts available now, but it is still undoubtedly beneficial to see a script performed before writing one. However, six of the nineteen students in the literature course did not see either performance, and only three students saw both performed. I am led to conclude that, although helpful, a performance of a script while the students are writing is not requisite to the success of the project in a dramatic literature class.

There is no reason why the writing and acting projects could not become one project for a single class. The value of this particular experiment, however, was that acting students, who are always looking for new and different material, learned about literature through the performance of educational scripts, one of which was written by a fellow student, while literature students in turn learned about literature through writing and structuring its material for performance. Whatever the organization of such an experiment, it seems certain that students as well as teachers can be successful in the development and production of educational scripts that teach literature through performance. The potential for creative activity is immense, and the result of the activity is the growth and development of the student-as-artist.

ON TOUR WITH *A CANTERBURY CAPER*

by Lynn Morrow

Through techniques of improvisation and creative problem solving, a body of literature can be translated into a viable and dynamic theatrical performance. I had long been fascinated by the educational possibilities in such a presentation, but it was through my four-year association with the teacher/artists of THE COLLECTION that I came to fully perceive the learning potential for both actor and audience in the performance of literature.

In preparing Albright College's production of *A Canterbury Caper* which would tour during a January Interim, a time primarily devoted to nontraditional studies and experimental teaching, we did not begin with the script. As a matter of fact, the thirteen students involved neither saw a script nor were advised of its specific content until three weeks after we started work. We began instead with a rather standard workshop on improvisation. In my experience the process of improvising literature releases a creative vitality in students which is essential to their transformation into student/artists. Such improvisation allows the student to explore character and action outside the confines of a preconceived notion of drama as representational and linear.

Though the first improvisational exercises involved only two or three people, we moved rapidly to exercises involving the whole group. A majority of these group improvisations required the students to create an atmosphere and/or an environment in which an action was to take place. We also experimented with some poetry. After discussing the poem, the students attempted to dramatize its meaning or feeling with physical movement and vocal expression. Meanwhile the students, most of whom had not read Chaucer's *The Canterbury Tales* at all, had been asked to read The Wife of Bath's prologue and tale, an improvised performance of which was the final project of the workshop sessions.

Confronted with the literature in linear form, the students created a series of vignettes depicting the Wife of Bath's relationship with her various husbands and a separate piece comprised of scenes from her tale. It is significant that they chose the theater for their performance, though the workshop had been conducted in a rehearsal room. They needed the curtains to indicate the beginning and end of each vignette and to hide performers yet to appear.

In discussing what they had done, the students agreed that their improvisation had lacked unity of action and was far too long and dull. Yet Chaucer had not been dull. We turned to Chaucer and his creation of the Wife of Bath for the answer. It was decided that the long preamble to her tale, in which she details her relationship with various husbands, was not simply an autobiographical exposé to entertain her companions — they seem to weary of it soon enough — but rather a displaying of herself, her wealth, her sexual prowess, and her good nature in order to attract yet another husband. Thus the Wife of Bath's objective or action, to get another husband, becomes the unifying factor of the piece. In the light of the Wife's objective, her tale can be seen as not simply a message to all men but also as a lesson for a potential sixth husband upon how he may live happily ever after with her. Through Chaucer's art, The Wife of Bath reveals more, of course, than she intends; hence the action is colored by her unconscious objective, which is to rule her man without loss of his love. The "we lived happily ever after" nature of her account of her final relationship with her fifth husband in the prologue as well as the fairytale nature of her story may also be seen then as an expression of her fantasies.

The students were asked to redo their improvisational performance using our discussion for guidance and working under the following conditions: everyone was to be on stage and involved at all times; the action was to be continuous without stops and starts; the Wife of Bath's objective was to be a central consideration for the entire action. Though the actress was cautioned to "play" only conscious objectives, how they were to be played could be colored by the perception of the unconscious ones as well. The students' solutions to these creative problems were interestingly quite similar to those THE COLLECTION had devised in their production.

Scripts were then distributed, and readings were held for eight of the thirteen students who wished to perform while technical responsibilities were assigned to the others. Although the original production was done with five performers, there were distinct visual advantages in using eight. The parts were, of course, distributed differently, one actor for example playing Alison and the Fox, another The Host, Absolom and the Christian Boy. The performers were given several days to learn the first act, at which time we began our work on the script. Our discussions of Chaucer continued, but we only used improvisation occasionally to solve particular creative problems. Like THE COLLECTION we used ladders and pillows for settings and properties, and the final production was similar in effect to the original — though even more athletic.

In the months to come members of our audiences often remarked that we were lucky to have such creative, poised, and experienced young performers. It wasn't luck. It was the dedication and hard work of these students, whose majors ranged from pre-med to social science, coupled with improvisational experimentation, and Chaucer that turned them into student/artists. And as they began their four-week tour which would bring *A Canterbury Caper* to some twenty-five hundred high school students, they were not unlike pilgrims themselves.

On a cold, crisp morning in January, the group of young people crowded three ladders, an array of pillows, a suitcase of costumes, a guitar, and themselves into the twelve-passenger van that over the next few weeks was to carry them 2,300 miles to twenty-one high schools in Eastern Pennsylvania and Rhode Island. They had been preceded two hours earlier by members of the technical crew who carried with them the nine-by-twelve green rug around which the blocking of *A Canterbury Caper* was oriented. The size of the stage would determine whether the movement would be spread out or tightened, but it would always be done in relationship to the rug. By now, the crew would have taped the rug in place and would be setting up whatever lighting was available and learning the light board — of necessity the lighting was kept simple.

As the van pulled away from Albright College, the cast nervously speculated on how their performance would be received by the college-bound juniors and seniors at the first school at which we performed. Had they read Chaucer? If not, did it matter? There would be a few surprises either way. The joy and the life the performers had discovered in Chaucer's materials and their own acquired enthusiasm for the *Tales* would surely carry across the footlights. But would the high school audiences be quiet for the Prioress' opening prayer after the humor and chaos of The Miller's Tale? During rehearsals, the cast had feared that the opening argument between Chanticleer and Pertelote in The Nuns' Priest's Tale was too pedantic and dull, but so far the adult audiences had been delighted with it. How would the high school audience respond?

The students ruefully remembered the letter the group had received from an English professor at a community college in New York where they had performed at a recent theater festival. The letter had questioned the wisdom of presenting an author who made sexual deeds and misdeeds so central to his work to youngsters. The performers, most of whom were only months away from being high school students themselves, were secure in their knowledge that the students who read *The Canterbury Tales* would be curiously awaiting the portrayal of them, and that those students who had not as yet been introduced to Chaucer would be favorably disposed toward this renowned author of the "pious" Middle Ages. But they were concerned over the charge in the letter that the presentation of The Prioress' Tale would foster anti-semitic feelings in the undiscriminating youngster who would be unlikely to place the tale in a proper framework. It could only be hoped that the performances would so emphasize the juxtaposition of the prologue's description of the dainty Prioress with her delicate sensibilities with her brutal, bloodcurdling tale that the audience could not help but perceive the irony inherent in her character.

In the weeks to come there would not be a single reference made by any student or teacher to anti-semitism in the production. In one high school the Headmaster considered stopping the production at intermission because of the sexual content of *The Tales*, and as a result one junior high school booking was cancelled, but considering the obvious enthusiasm of the eight hundred students enjoying Chaucer it was decided that to continue was the lesser of two evils. The performance was continued as was the tour.

The touring group's fears and concerns expressed that first day abated with each performance and disappeared after they played their first inner-city school. Upon congratulating the company the head of the English Department had remarked: "If you can play successfully to these students from this school on a Friday afternoon, you can play to anyone, anywhere at any time." So the pilgrim-artists continued to wend their way with a surer understanding that good performances make good audiences and that good audiences enhance those performances. While the student/artists were using an educational script and teaching Chaucer to other students through their performance, they were consistently learning themselves through the interaction that is so essential to both dramatic and educational experience.

NOTES

1. Thomas J. Cottle, *Time's Children: Impressions of Youth* (Boston: Little Brown and Co., 1971); p. 96.

2. See Bradley Morison, "The Artist as Teacher," *Saturday Review*, 19 December 1970, p. 51.

3. Richard Courtney, *Play, Drama, and Thought: The Intellectual Background to Drama Education*, 3rd Rev. Ed. (New York: Drama Book Specialists, 1974), p. 129. Courtney speaks of actor-teachers trained by Brian Way in his "London Theatre Centre" and of "Theater-in-Education" groups of actor-teachers attached to professional adult theaters in England. Although student groups of performers often tour in an educational capacity in the United States, perhaps the unique aspect of THE COLLECTION in this country is its use of teachers rather than students or actors as the performers.

4. Aristotle, *Aristotle's Poetics*. Tr. by S. H. Butcher with an Introduction by Francis Fergusson (New York, Hill and Wang, 1961), p. 55

5. John Dewey, *Experience and Education* (New York: Collier Books, 1973), pp. 46, 59, 85; John Dewey; *Art as Experience* (New York: Minton, Balch & Co., 1934), pp. 7, 8, 52, 54.

6. William Shakespeare, "Hamlet," *The Riverside Shakespeare*. Textual ed. G. Blakemore Evans (Boston: Houghton Mifflin Co., 1974), pp. 1161-1162.

7. A brief, student-made film (eighteen minutes long) called "Shakespeare's Mirror" may be rented from the Ohio State University Film Department at Haskett Hall. The film shows THE COLLECTION rehearsing *Shakespeare's Mirror*, performing sections of it, and discussing it in post-sessions with audiences.

8. THE COLLECTION'S solutions to such problems are meant only to be suggestive since each performing group will doubtless find its own creative approach to the material.

9. Shakespeare, "Hamlet," *The Riverside Shakespeare*, pp. 1161-1162.

10. Shakespeare, "As You Like It," *The Riverside Shakespeare*, p. 381.

11. "Our need in the post-Brecht theatre, is to find a way forward, back to Shakespeare." Peter Brook, *The Empty Space* (New York: Avon Books, 1968), p. 78.

12. *Shakespeare's Mirror* gave me the opportunity to put into practice techniques that I had studied for two years (1962-1964) in William Ball's Classical Workshop in New York City. I remember how striking it was to me when Mr. Ball first worked with us on following the rhythms designated by Shakespeare, cutting out pauses that were not indicated, and keeping our thoughts up with what was happening on the line, "thinking on the line," he called it.

13. See p.   for a discussion of Aristotle on imitation.

14. Shakespeare, "King Lear," *The Riverside Shakespeare*, p. 1263.

15. See The Appendix, pp. 85-97, for a discussion of student performances of *A Canterbury Caper*. See also a drama anthology by Mark S. Auburn and Katherine H. Burkman, *Drama Through Performance* (Boston: Houghton Mifflin Co., 1977), for specific ways in which informal student performance of scenes in the classroom may be integrated with the study of dramatic literature.

16. See Kenneth Burke's *A Grammar of Motives* (Berkeley and Los Angeles: University of California Press, 1969) and Francis Fergusson's *The Idea of a Theatre: A Study of Ten Plays* (Princeton: Princeton University Press, 1949).

17. *Aristotle's Poetics*, p. 62.

18. pp. 155 and 158. All critics do not agree with Kittredge's view of *The Canterbury Tales* as essentially dramatic in structure, but a book by R. M. Lumiansky, *Of Sondry Folk: The Dramatic Principle in The Canterbury Tales* (Austin: University of Texas Press, 1955), supports this contention.

19. THE COLLECTION'S use of ladders and pillows (not unlike the varied uses of stools as everything from dancing partners to logs in *Shakespeare's Mirror*) is only meant to be suggestive. As with the Shakespeare script, performance groups will find their own creative uses for the properties. Indeed, a very different but very effective version of *The Canterbury Tales* was conceived and directed by Marya Bednerik at the University of Massachusetts at Amherst just prior to THE COLLECTION'S endeavor. This production employed a large cast and a setting with a huge tree and properties that all suggested stained glass windows.

20. Note the non-linear use of the prologue material in the script, designed to enhance the comic and dramatic effect of the Wife of Bath's rather lengthy prologue to her tale. Perched on top of a ladder, the Wife's fifth husband reads from a pillow-as-book about the evil ways of women, constantly interrupting the Wife's account of her several marriages and providing a counterpoint to them.

21. See Appendix, pp. 85-97.

22. William F. Pinar and Madeleine R. Grumet, *Toward a Poor Curriculum: An Introduction to the Theory and Practice of Currere* (Dubuque, Iowa: Kendall/Hunt Publishing Co., 1976), p. 75.

23. Francis Fergusson, *The Idea of a Theatre,* pp. 5, 10, 276.

24. The playwright, according to Aristotle, should "place the scene as far as possible, before his eyes" when he creates, and should use "appropriate gestures; for those who feel emotions are most convincing through natural sympathy with the characters they represent; and one who is agitated storms, one who is angry rages with the most lifelike reality. Hence poetry implies either a happy gift of nature or a strain of madness. In the one case a man can take the mold of any character; in the other, he is lifted out of his proper self." *Aristotle's Poetics,* pp. 87-88.

25. Constantin Stanislavski, *An Actor Prepares.* tr. by Elizabeth Reynolds Hapgood (New York: Theatre Arts Books, 1970); pp. 14, 37, 48, 49, 110, 111.

26. Pinar and Grumet, *Toward a Poor Curriculum,* p. 87.

SELECTED BIBLIOGRAPHY

Aristotle. *Aristotle's Poetics.* Translated by S. H. Butcher with an Introduction by Francis Fergusson. New York: Hill and Wang, A Dramabook, 1961.

Auburn, Mark S.; Burkman, Katherine H.; and Munday, Mildred B. "Classroom Performance in the Teaching of Dramatic Literature: Some Observations on an Experiment." *New Directions in Teaching* 4 (1974): 10-19.

Auburn, Mark S.; and Burkman, Katherine H. *Drama Through Performance.* Boston: Houghton Mifflin Co., 1977.

Barber, C. L. *Shakespeare's Festive Comedy.* Cleveland and New York: Meridian Books, 1963.

Bertram, Joseph. *Acting Shakespeare.* London: Routledge & Paul, 1960.

Brook, Peter. *The Empty Space.* New York: Avon Books, 1968.

Burke, Kenneth. *A Grammar of Motives.* Berkeley and Los Angeles: University of California Press, 1969.

Chaucer, Geoffrey. *The Canterbury Tales* in *The Portable Chaucer.* Selected, translated, and edited by Theodore Morrison. New York: The Viking Press, 1949.

Cottle, Thomas J. *Time's Children: Impressions of Youth.* Boston: Little Brown and Co., 1971.

Courtney, Richard. *Play, Drama and Thought: The Intellectual Background To Drama in Education.* 3rd rev. ed. New York: Drama Book Specialist/ Publishers, 1974.

Dewey, John. *Art as Experience.* New York: Minton, Balch & Co., 1934.

———. *Experience and Education.* New York: Collier Books, 1973.

Fergusson, Francis. *Shakespeare: The Pattern in His Carpet.* New York: Delacorte Press, 1949.

———. *The Idea of a Theatre: A Study of Ten Plays.* Princeton: Princeton University Press, 1949. (First paperback ed., 1968.)

Gilbert, Miriam. "Teaching Dramatic Literature." *Educational Theatre Journal* (1973): 83-94.

Kittredge, George Lyman. *Chaucer and His Poetry.* Cambridge, Mass.: Harvard University Press, 1967.

Lumiansky, Robert Mayer. *Of Sondry Folk: The Dramatic Principle in The Canterbury Tales.* Austin: University of Texas Press, 1955.

Morison, Bradley. "The Artist as Teacher." *Saturday Review,* 19 December 1970, p. 51.

Parry, Christopher. *English Through Drama: A Way of Teaching.* Cambridge: Cambridge University Press, 1972.

Pinar, William F. and Grumet, Madeleine R. *Toward a Poor Curriculum: An Introduction to the Theory and Practice of Currere.* Dubuque, Iowa: Kendall/Hunt Publishing Co., 1976.

Rosenberg, Helane S; and Fennelly, Lawrence W. "The Actor/Teacher: A New Idea from Britain." *Education* 96 (1975) 50-53.

Seyler, Athene; and Haggard, Stephen. *The Craft of Comedy.* New York: Theatre Arts Books, 1946.

Shakespeare, William. *The Riverside Shakespeare.* Textual ed. G. Blakemore Evans. Boston: Houghton Mifflin Co., 1974.

Stanislavski, Constantin. *An Actor Prepares.* Translated by Elizabeth Reynolds Hapgood. New York: Theatre Arts Books, 1970.